AN ESSAY
IN AUTOBIOGRAPHY

By the Same Author

DOCTOR ZHIVAGO

Boris Pasternak to-day

BORIS PASTERNAK

An Essay in Autobiography

With an Introduction by
Edward Crankshaw

Collins and Harvill Press
LONDON
1959

Translated from the Russian by
Manya Harari

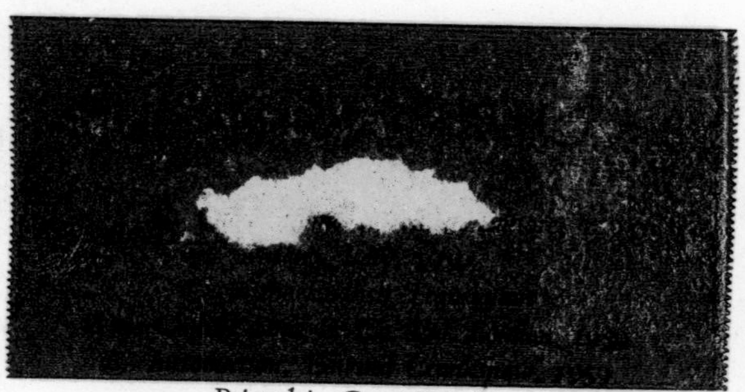

Printed in Great Britain
Collins Clear-Type Press : London & Glasgow

CONTENTS

Acknowledgments

The publishers are grateful to Sir Maurice Bowra for permission to reproduce passages from his book *The Creative Experiment*, MacMillan & Co.

They would also like to acknowledge their gratitude to Mrs. L. Slater for her permission to reproduce the portraits opposite pages 33, 48, 49, 64, 65, 80, 81 and 96, to the Ashmolean Museum, Oxford, for permission to reproduce the drawing opposite page 32, and to Express News and Feature Services for permission to reproduce a photograph of the author both as a frontispiece and on the wrapper of the book. The photographic copyright of the illustrations opposite pages 49, 80, 81, 96 belongs to the Pushkin Club and that of the illustrations opposite pages 33, 48, 64, 65 to *The Times*.

LIST OF PLATES

All the illustrations, except the two photographs, are from portraits by the author's father Leonid Pasternak

Introduction by Edward Crankshaw

IN 1954 there was a plan to publish in Moscow a collection of Pasternak's poems. This was during the first "thaw," which followed Stalin's death in March 1953. During the summer and autumn of that year there was a deep stirring among the writers, the painters, the musicians of the Soviet Union. Wild things were said and great dreams were dreamed. It was no longer necessary for Western sympathisers to speculate about the secret feelings of the Soviet intelligentsia during the last years of Stalin's rule: they told us themselves, sometimes with frightening candour. For example, in the published record of the meeting of the dramatists' section of the Union of Soviet Writers held in October 1953 there could be read harsher and more radical criticism of the blighting influence of Stalin and Zhdanov on the creative arts than anything written in the West.

Writers, long dead, were at least partly rehabilitated and their works brought out in new editions. Still living writers, long silent, were encouraged to speak again. Chief among these was Pasternak. In April 1954 ten of the poems written for his novel, *Doctor Zhivago*, were printed in *Novy Mir*, the literary monthly which was, two years later, to make new history by publishing Dudintsev's controversial novel, *Not by Bread Alone*.

Doctor Zhivago itself was not submitted for publication until the summer of 1956. In September the typescript was returned with a very long and reasoned letter, which was not published until the great row about the Nobel Prize in the autumn of 1958, two years later. There was no violence in that letter of rejection, at any rate in the form in which it has been given to the world, and although quite clearly it was prompted, at least in part, by individuals hostile to Pasternak and perhaps jealous of the special position he occupied in the hearts of Russian readers and in the estimation of his foreign colleagues, the spirit of the rejection as a whole was closer to sorrow than to anger. At any rate, until well into 1957 it was still hoped that *Doctor Zhivago* might be published in the Soviet Union if Pasternak would agree to make certain alterations. Even as late as that, *Novy Mir* published more of his poems. And when, in the same year, the Italian publisher Feltrinelli, brought out the first translation of the novel against the express wishes of Alexey Surkov, Secretary of the

Soviet Writers' Union, Pasternak was not made to suffer. These facts should be born in mind by all those, and they are many, who speak as though there had been a total reversion to Zhdanovism in the cultural life of the Soviet Union.

It was not until the Swedish Academy fatefully decided to award the Nobel Prize to Pasternak that the storm broke loose. Then he was solemnly expelled from the Writers' Union and a number of the most undesirable characters in the land started using the language of the gutter. At this moment there seems to have been a determined effort to drive Pasternak into exile. " He is free to leave when he likes. Let him receive his contemptible prize. He need not come back! "

But Pasternak, sixty-eight years old, who had endured a life-time of suffering of an intensity inconceivable to us, refused to meet his persecutors half-way. Already once, in 1937, he had defied Stalin's fury by refusing to put his signature to a document approving the execution of Marshal Tukhachevsky and others. He had survived because nobody had been brave enough to report this defiance. Now, nearly twenty years later, he had finally declared himself in a book which had swept the world. He was evidently in a mood to stand by it, though it killed him; and if killing was not the order of the day in Khrushchev's Russia (as, indeed, it is not), then he, Pasternak, was not going to allow himself, so long as he could help it, to be conveniently shipped abroad and then held up as a traitor to his country. So, as we know, he renounced the Nobel Prize and addressed a personal letter to Mr. Khrushchev asking to be allowed to stay. No reply to that letter was ever published; but the outcry was dropped overnight.

This, no doubt, is an over-simplification. There were other and more personal reasons for Pasternak's desire to live as long as he was allowed, and die, in his own land—cost what it might in suffering and privation. But it is important to grasp the real point. It is important because he has since been accused in the West, either through stupidity or malice, of cowardice in his clinging to Russia, in his refusal, so long as refusal lies in his power, to follow so many of his contemporaries from his own and other lands into the bitterness of exile. No charge was ever shabbier or wider of the mark. *Doctor Zhivago* is more than a book; it is an expression of life. In his terrible and self-imposed isolation, with hands outstretched towards him from all over the world, Pasternak goes on living that life.

I have spoken of this because Pasternak in his *Essay in Autobiography* has nothing to say about it, or about the collapse of the plan to publish his collected poems. This Essay was written as an introduction to the collection. So it must be seen as a fragment of a book. The poems must wait. The fragment, however, stands by itself. It is autobiographical only in the spiritual sense. It tells us next to nothing about the physical circumstances of Pasternak's life and very little—though enough for the attentive ear—about his anguish of mind. It does, however, tell us a great deal about the sort of man Pasternak is and the influences which culminated in the novel which he himself regards as his life's fulfilment.

Pasternak is sixty-nine. His first poems were published in the autumn of 1914, when he was twenty-four. Because of an injury to his leg in a riding accident he was not called up when war broke out, and he continued to publish until 1932. There was no more original work then, but many translations, until 1943, when he broke his silence with some war poems. In 1946, with Zhdanov's savage attack on "cosmopolitanism," he fell silent again and did not speak until after Stalin's death, in 1954. But during these long periods of silence, which were self-imposed, one of eleven years, one of eight years, he was a venerated figure, seen as being above the battle, discovered by generation after generation of Soviet youth and passed on to the next, like a torch.

He was not above the battle. He was active and fighting all the time. But the battle he was fighting was his own. While others were fighting with more or less integrity the battle for survival, the battle to be heard and yet to preserve a remnant of their private vision (as though vision were divisible), Pasternak was fighting the battle for truth. When he could speak the truth as he saw it, he spoke; when it was physically impossible for him to speak the truth he was silent.

He was not alone in this battle for the truth; but he is alone among living Soviet writers in having fought it unremittingly and without compromise to the wonderful, the miraculous end, when his Truth suddenly and shatteringly broke through every barrier to flood the world. It does not matter what happens to Boris Pasternak after that, and he must know it, thankfully. He has achieved the impossible. He has spoken from the bottom of a deep pit and his words have been clearly heard. He is the first effective martyr of modern times, in a world which seemed to have made an end of martyrdom by the simple process of drowning it in darkness.

The fact of Pasternak's life-long battle for truth, and his recognition since the late twenties as a man set apart, is important to-day because there is a strong movement to conceal it. Innocent visitors to the Soviet Union will be told with disarming plausibility that until the fuss about *Zhivago* very few people had ever heard of his poetry, which appealed only to lovers of the perverse and esoteric. This is categorically untrue. Even at the first Writers' Congress in 1934, when Pasternak, silent for two years, was sharply assailed for his wrong-headed attitude towards the Sovietisation of art, he was publicly acclaimed as a master, and his poetry was in fact quite astonishingly popular. It seems fairly clear that even those who thought of him as being above the battle must have known in their hearts that in fact he was fighting his own battle, which was also really theirs, and what it was about. Because of the language difficulty his public outside Russia was naturally more limited. I suppose the majority of English-speaking readers owe their discovery of his poetry to Sir Maurice Bowra, who made many beautiful translations of individual poems and who introduced him as a major figure in his book, *The Creative Experiment*, published just eleven years ago. This volume contains an introductory chapter and six separate essays on Cavafy, Appollinaire, Mayakovsky, Pasternak, Eliot, Lorca and Alberti. It is indispensable for every reader who wishes to know what lies behind *Doctor Zhivago*. It is all the more remarkable in its prophetic insight since it is confined to those poems written before 1923, when Pasternak was thirty-three.

Listen to the closing passage:

> " Pasternak responds to the special character of his calling with a special sense of the responsibilities which it puts upon him. He believes, above all, that everything he writes must be a work of art, complete and independent with its own life, the final vehicle by which experience is selected and organised and transformed into a permanent shape. He also believes that no work of art has any value unless it is true in a rigorous and exacting sense, true not merely to fact but to experience, to all that the poet sees in it and feels about it. This double ideal is perhaps responsible for his complexities and roughnesses, but it is no less responsible for his final success and for his special importance. In a revolutionary age Pasternak has seen beyond the disturbed surface of things to the powers behind it and found there an explanation of what really matters in the world. Through his unerring sense of poetry he has reached to the wide issues and shown that the creative calling, with its efforts and its frustrations and its unanticipated

triumphs, is, after all, something profoundly natural and closely related to the sources of life."

Those words, written long before we had any reason to suppose that Pasternak would ever write a novel, and based on the poetry of his earliest years, could serve well as a comment on *Doctor Zhivago*. Re-reading them now, in the light of what has happened since Sir Maurice Bowra wrote them down, it seems to me that not the least of the services Sir Maurice has done is to demonstrate, when it is most needed, that, to adapt his own phrases, "the critical calling, with its efforts and frustrations and its unanticipated triumphs, is, after all, something profoundly natural and closely related to the sources of art." Sir Maurice Bowra, too, has had his own triumph and his vindication—which is also a triumph and a vindication for his calling.

This is not irrelevant. Listen to Pasternak himself:

"I dislike my style up to 1940, just as I quarrel with half of Mayakovsky's writings and with some of Yesenin's. I dislike the disintegrating forms, the impoverished thought and the littered and uneven language of those days." And again : "I would not lift a finger to rescue more than a quarter of my writings from oblivion." And again: "The poems scattered over the past years of my life . . . are steps preparatory to the novel."

Yet to one critic the essence of the novel was implicit in the preparatory steps; and to thousands of readers it was sensed in them. This tells us something about creative writers too, and about Pasternak in particular. It is worth holding on to this fact as we read Pasternak on himself.

He had written an "experiment in autobiography" as far back as the twenties, *Safe Conduct*, long out of print in Russia. This new Essay was intended to supersede *Safe Conduct*, which, Pasternak insists, "was spoiled by its affected manner, the besetting sin of those days." He seems to have spent thirty years atoning for the "affectations" of the first part of his life, driven unresistingly by the demand for total directness and truth, a directness and truth which had yet been detected in his earliest work, through all the surface imperfections, by countless readers. The fruit of those years, which have purged away so many imperfections and all traces of the egocentric, is a great novel, some poems and this short essay.

About this *Essay in Autobiography* I have nothing direct to say. It is here between these covers, wonderfully slight and unbelievably strong, with each sentence built to carry the weight of a lifetime's experience. Here, distilled, is the essence of a great writer and a great man, solid, and yet so volatile that it evades analysis and vanishes into thin air, like a butterfly cupped in the hands, like the elusiveness of life itself. For a Russian the whole thing is crystal clear, but because so many of the names which appear in it, because the whole background of Pasternak's life, are unfamiliar to most English readers, it is perhaps justifiable to dwell for a moment on that background.

The young Pasternak was cradled in the arts. His father, Leonid, was a painter of considerable gifts and reputation, the friend of countless painters and writers and musicians; his mother was Rosa Kaufman, a concert pianist, who had been a child prodigy. When Boris was thirteen his parents became summer neighbours of the composer Scriabin, who was also the uncle of the man who was to become Stalin's right-hand, Molotov, born Scriabin. In childhood Pasternak's sensitivity to music had been acute, and Scriabin's music swept him on a swift upcurrent into the higher atmosphere: music was to be his life. It is permissible to believe that Scriabin was very much in his mind when Pasternak was creating the character of Uncle Kolya in *Doctor Zhivago*. And it is worth remembering in this context that Scriabin is one of those composers who do not export well. To most musical Russians he means a very great deal. Scriabin touches in them a dominant chord which, vibrating intolerably, overwhelms the defects of his music—perhaps as Bruckner does for the Austrians.

The young Pasternak was going to be a great composer, relying on inspiration and perfect spontaneity. Everyone was pleased. He had no struggle to get his destiny as an artist accepted by his family: they expected nothing else. His struggle began only when, a little later, he began to understand the seriousness of art. Then, he tells us, from one moment to the next, he threw overboard his pretensions as a musician. The poet, the battler for truth, for the first time stirred within him.

It occurs to me that through the arrangement of these pages I may have given too much emphasis to that aspect of Pasternak's life-long conflict which may be summed up as the battle between the individual and overweening Authority. If so, this can be immediately corrected. Pasternak's first and last battle was with himself and with his artistic environment: it was only in 1932, with the subordination of literature in the Soviet Union to the ideals and disciplines of RAPP, the Russian Association of Proletarian Writers, forerunner of the notorious

Writers' Union, that he embarked on his battle with Authority. He was then forty-two.

The second decade of the century in Russia was not an easy time for learning self-discipline. After the Russian collapse in the war with Japan and the striking, rioting and killing of 1905, the sense of impending disintegration was overwhelmingly strong, and among the Russian intelligentsia, battering their heads against the last convulsive stonewalling of the autocracy, it found expression in violently individualistic self-assertion. The mood was common to all Europe in those last years before the 1914 war blew the old culture finally to bits: the futurists in Italy, the vorticists in England, the cubists in France, all formed separate expressions of a universal mood. All were tumbling over themselves to get rid of a past which still tenaciously hung on, and find new words, new images, for a new experience which, without their understanding it, was all too palpably lying in wait for them on the Somme, at Verdun, in the Dolomites, in the Masurian marshes, on the Field of Blackbirds—and in the streets and squares of Petersburg.

In Russia there were many different groups, each regarding itself as the unique repository of the truth, each more concerned with combating the pretensions of the others than with spontaneous creation. These occupied the ground which fell vacant after the collapse of Symbolism. For Alexander Blok, the leader of the Symbolists, the idol of pre-revolutionary youth, outlived the movement he stood for, and his last great revolutionary poems of 1918, "The Twelve" and "The Scythians," with their apocalyptic glitter, were very far removed from his early preoccupation with mystical love. All sought clarity and definition, as opposed to vague yearnings. Few found either.

By the time of the revolution the Futurists, with their absolute denial of the past and their urgent violence, were dominant. Their most gifted exponent was Mayakovsky, who was to kill himself in despair at the turn the revolution was taking in 1930, not without going half way to meet its demands, so that his bitter posthumous destiny was to see his later and cruder work seized upon by the men he could not live with and made part of the Stalinist canon—or, in the words of Pasternak: "Mayakovsky began to be introduced forcibly, like potatoes under Catherine the Great. This was his second death. He had no hand in it."

The two other most powerful movements were the Acmeists and the Imagists. The main feature of the Imagist outlook was its stress on words and word associations and its contempt for matter and content.

In its extreme form, and influenced indirectly by Ezra Pound, Imagism abandoned sense altogether. They would have meant very little, but for the fact that a natural genius, Sergey Yesenin, allied himself with them and gave lustre to their company. Yesenin killed himself in 1925. The best of the Acmeists were its founder, Nikolay Gumilyov and the gentle Anna Akhmatova. Politically they were out of step with the times, and their emphasis was on clarity of expression and the reflection of real experience. Gumilyov was shot in 1921. Akhmatova survived, with long silences, to be one of the main targets of Zhdanov's savagery in 1946. She survived even that and is now being published once more.

It was against this background—there were countless other ceaselessly shifting groups—that the young Pasternak, full of confidence, first projected himself. And almost at once, without knowing quite why, he seemed to have realised that there was no place for him in any of these fiercely warring factions. To quote Sir Maurice Bowra again :

> " Each school suffered from exaggerating its claims. The Futurists' love of violence excluded many legitimate effects, the Acmeists were too traditional for a revolutionary age, and the Imagists spoiled their work by turning a means of

poetry into its chief end. What was needed was a poet who could pick up the different threads and turn the modern movements to meet modern needs without giving too much emphasis to this or that claim of the competing antagonists. The man appeared in Boris Pasternak."

After an early spell as a member of a small group called " Centrifuga " he began to walk by himself; and by 1927 he was the man we know to-day, standing apart equally from the excesses of so many of his colleagues and from the excesses of the State.

It is against this background that we read what he has to say about colleagues long dead. And it is against the background of Stalin's sustained effort to subordinate the arts to Party purposes that we must understand his long silences. From time to time a new and wonderful figure appears, only to die. The great majority of Soviet artists gave up the struggle in the early thirties. Some, like Leonid Leonov, tried for a time, and then retired, beaten. Mikhail Sholokhov, whose original version of *Quiet Flows the Don* (published in 1928, but long since expurgated) was the only great novel to be published in Soviet Russia until *Doctor Zhivago*, managed to keep going by not writing much and by compromising a good deal. Others threw themselves apparently heart and soul into the business of building Stalinism. Most took life as it came, with secret reservations. But Marina Tsvetayeva, Pasternak's idol, an original genius, who returned to the Soviet Union in 1939, was dead by her own hand in 1941. And Pasternak's two wonderful Georgians, Yashvili and Tabidze, both died in the thirties—Tabidze in one of the great purges, Yashvili by his own hand.

In 1956 it was the turn of the man who had so long been a pillar of Stalin's and Zhdanov's literary world, to kill himself: Alexander Fadeyev. So the wheel had turned full circle.

It is still turning. A few years ago it was thought a good idea to glorify Pasternak. Now he is in disgrace. But his voice has been heard, and will go on being heard, in a way which six years ago would have been inconceivable. And although he is silent, and although the Party is putting the screw on the arts once again, it seems in the highest degree improbable that the Soviet Union will have to suffer a return to pre-Zhivago days. All over Russia young poets and novelists are scribbling away, often in provincial towns which for decades have been neglected and suffered to rot; and what they are writing, though often crude, as often bears no discernible reference to the terms of art as laid down in Moscow. It is almost as if they had not heard the official summons. They will not be shot; most, we may hope, will not kill themselves in despair. And some at least will keep their souls. It looks better than it did in 1932 when Pasternak first stopped writing.

AN ESSAY
IN AUTOBIOGRAPHY

CHAPTER ONE

Early Childhood

IN *Safe Conduct*, an experiment in autobiography, written in the 'twenties, I described the circumstances which have shaped my life. Unfortunately, the book was spoiled by its affected manner, the besetting sin of those days.

I can't avoid retelling some of the events in the present sketch, but I will do my best not to repeat myself.

* * *

I was born in 1890 in Moscow, on the 29th of January according to the Old Calendar,[1] in Lyzhin's house opposite the Seminary in Oruzheiny Street. Surprisingly, something has remained in my memory of my walks in autumn with my wet-nurse [2] in the Seminary park—sodden paths heaped with fallen leaves, ponds and artificial hills, the painted Seminary railings, the noisy games and fights of the seminarists during their recreation.

Facing the gates of the Seminary there was a two-storeyed stone house; it had a courtyard for the cabbies, and our flat was above the vaulted archway of the courtyard entrance.

* * *

My impressions of my early childhood are made up of terrors and delights. They ascend in fairytale colours towards two central images which ruled my world and gave it unity: one is of the stuffed bears in the coachmakers' windows in Coachmakers Row; the other is of a kindly, shaggy, stooping giant with a deep toneless voice (this was the publisher Konchalovsky), and it includes his family, and their flat, and the pictures on its walls—sketches in pencil, wash and pen-and-ink, by Serov, Vrubel, my father and the brothers Vasnetsov.

Our neighbourhood was extremely sordid; it was close to the Fverskiye-Yamskiye, the Pipe and the lanes of the Jsvetnoy.[3] You were always being dragged away; you were not supposed to hear this, you were not allowed to know that. But sometimes nannies and wet-nurses wearied of isolation, and then we were surrounded by all sorts of company.

And at noon the mounted police drilled on the parade ground of the Znamensky Barracks.

As a result of all this rubbing shoulders with

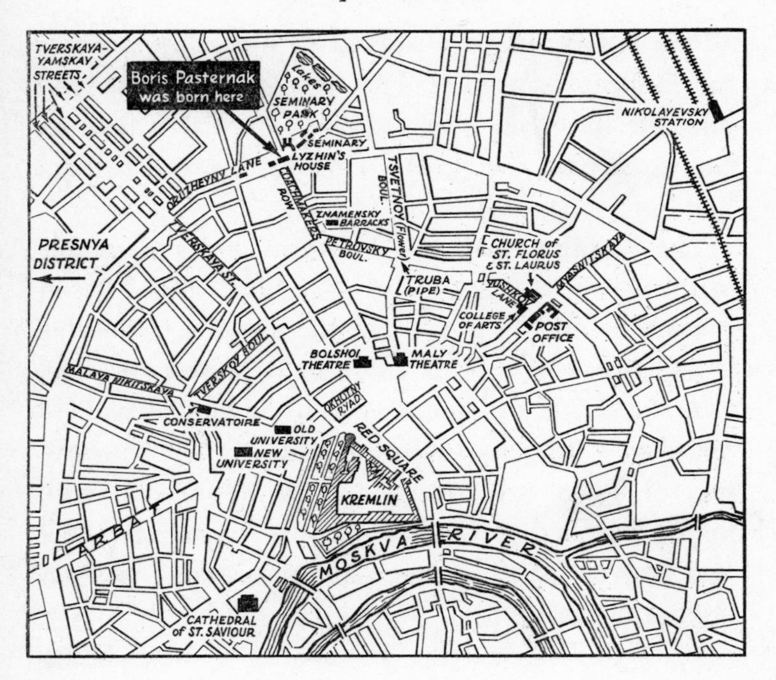

beggars and pilgrims, and of nearness to the world of the rejected and of listening to their stories of troubles and hysterics, I was filled too early and for life with a compassion for women, so terrible that it was hardly to be borne, and with a still more anguished pity for my parents who would die before me and whom it was my duty to deliver from the pains of hell by some shining deed, unheard-of and unique.

*　　　*　　　*

When I was three we moved to official quarters at the College of Arts.[4] This was in Myasnitskaya,[5] opposite the main Post Office. Our flat was in an annexe across the yard, separate from the main building.

The building was old, beautiful and remarkable in many ways. The fire of 1812[6] had spared it. A century before our time under the Empress Catherine, it had been the secret refuge of a Masonic Lodge. One corner, at the intersection of Myasnitskaya and Yushkov Lane, had a pillared, semi-circular balcony; part of it formed a recess and communicated with the College hall. From it, you could have a clear view of the Myasnitskaya running into the distance towards the railway stations.

From this balcony the inhabitants of the building watched the funeral procession of the Emperor Alexander III in 1894 and two years later saw part of the festivities in honour of the coronation of Nicholas II.

Standing near the balustrade, among a crowd of students and professors, my mother held me up in her arms. An abyss opened at her feet. At the bottom of it was the empty roadway strewn with sand. The street waited, holding its breath. Officers bustled about, shouting orders in loud voices, but they were inaudible to the onlookers on the balcony,

Boris Pasternak as a boy, 1898

Nurse

as if the stillness of the breathless thousands whom the soldiers kept pushing from the roadway back on to the edges of the kerb had swallowed up the sounds, like sand swallowing water. Slowly, mournfully, the bells rang out. A wave gathered out of the distance and rolled past into the distance beyond, stirring a sea of hands as Moscow bared its head and crossed itself. To the sound of bells tolling on every side, the procession advanced endlessly—troops, clergy, horses plumed and draped in black, a catafalque of inconceivable magnificence and heralds in the curious costumes of a bygone age. On they went, past houses muffled and upholstered in black; the funeral flags hung downcast.

The spirit of pomp and ceremony was inseparable from the College which was under the ægis of the Ministry of the Imperial Court. The Grand Duke Sergey Alexandrovich was its patron and he came regularly to its exhibitions and its speech days. The Grand Duke was thin and lanky. Shielding their sketch-books with their hats, Serov and my father drew caricatures of him at the receptions which he attended at the Golitsins' and Yakunchikovs.'

* * *

Facing the wicket-gate of a small garden shaded by ancient trees, the annexe where we lived rose above the sheds and offices in the yard. Hot lunches were served to students in the basement, and an everlasting smell of fried cutlets and pasties cooked in batter hung over the stairs. Our flat was on the first landing. The College Clerk lived on the floor above.

Half a century later, I read the following under the heading "1894" on page 125 of a recent Soviet book, *Moscow in the Life and Work of Leo Tolstoy* by N. S. Rodionov:

> On the 23rd November, Tolstoy and his daughters went to a concert given at the flat of the painter Leonid Pasternak, Director of the College of Arts. The musicians were Pasternak's wife, the 'cellist Brandukov and the violinist Grzhimaldi, both Professors at the Conservatoire.

This is true except for one small error. The Director of the College was not my father but Prince Lvov.

I remember that evening perfectly. I had been put to bed, but late in the night I was aroused by such a sweet, nostalgic torment as I had not experienced in the same degree before. I cried out and wept in fear and anguish. But the music drowned my cries and it was not until the end of the movement that anyone heard me. Then the curtain which hung across the room, dividing it in two, was pushed aside.

My mother came in, bent over me and soon calmed me down. She may have carried me into the drawing-room, or perhaps I only saw it through the open door. The air was filled with cigarette smoke; the candles blinked as if it stung their eyes. They shone on the red varnished wood of the 'cello and of the violin. The piano loomed black. The men were in black frock-coats. Women leaned out of their shoulder-high dresses like flowers out of flower baskets. Like smoke rings, the grey-ringed heads of two or three old men drifted together. One of them was the painter Gué, whom I was later to know well and see often. The image of another has been present to me, as to most people, all my life: to me especially because my father illustrated his work, went to see him, honoured him, and indeed our whole house was permeated by his spirit. This was Lev Nikolayevich[7]. . . .

Why then did I cry so bitterly and why do I remember my anxiety so well? I was used to the sound of the piano—my mother was an accomplished pianist; to me it was inseparable from that of music itself. But the voices of strings—particularly strings combined in chamber music—were unfamiliar and as disturbing as if they had been real voices carried through the open window from the street, calling for help and announcing a disaster.

It was, I think, the winter of two deaths—Anton Rubinstein's and Chaikovsky's.[8] The music was probably Chaikovsky's famous "Trio".

That evening marked for me the end of my unconscious early childhood. From then on, my memory functioned and my consciousness was active and unbroken by long gaps, as in an adult.

* * *

Every spring the Travelling Exhibition[9] was held in the College show rooms. The pictures arrived from Petersburg in the winter and were stored in sheds—there was a row of them outside our back windows. A little before Easter the crates were brought out into the yard. The College servants prised them open and unscrewed the heavy picture frames from the boards; then each picture was carried by two men across the yard to the main building. Perched on the window-sills we watched excitedly. That was how we first saw many pictures by Russian masters,[10] which to-day are famous and make up half the contents of the public galleries and State collections.

It was only at the beginning that the group of painters[11] with whom my father was connected took part in these shows. Later they founded their own younger associations, "The Union of Russian Artists". [12]

In the late 'nineties the sculptor Pavel Trubetskoy, who had spent his life in Italy, arrived in Moscow. A studio with a glass roof was built on to the back of our house and put at his disposal. Our kitchen window which used to look out on the yard now looked into his workroom. Through it we could watch him and his caster, Robecco, at work, and see his models—not only children and ballerinas, but mounted Cossacks and even carriages and pairs which drove easily into the lofty studio through its wide gateway.

It was also from our kitchen that my father's remarkable illustrations to Tolstoy's *Resurrection* were dispatched.

The novel appeared, chapter by chapter in *Niva*,[13] a periodical edited by the Petersburg publisher Marx. It came out regularly and on time. My father worked feverishly to meet the deadline.

But Tolstoy often held up the proofs and altered them so much that the drawings made for the original version had to be changed. Luckily Father's notebooks were filled with sketches of the courtrooms, transit prisons,[14] villages and trains which formed so many of Tolstoy's backgrounds. This stock of living details and the realism which he shared with Tolstoy allowed him to keep close to the text.

To save time, the drawings were sent off by hand as occasion offered. The guards on the express trains to Petersburg acted as messengers. My imagination was impressed by the sight of a uniformed guard waiting outside our kitchen door, as on a station platform outside a railway carriage.

Joiner's glue sizzled on the range. The drawings were hastily sprinkled with fixative and glued on sheets of cardboard, and the parcels, wrapped up, tied and sealed, were handed over to the guard.

CHAPTER TWO

Scriabin

THE second decade of my life was very different from the first. Moscow in the 'nineties, in all the splendour of her "sixteen hundred belfries", [1] still had the look of a remote, provincial town as picturesque as in a fairytale, but with something of the legendary grandeur of the ancient capital and of the Third Rome.[2] Ancient customs were still observed. In the autumn, horses were blessed in Yushkov Lane which ran between the College and the Church of St. Florus and St. Laurus,[3] who were regarded as patrons of horse-breeders; the horses and the grooms and coachmen who brought them crowded the church precincts and the Lane as if it were a horse fair.

It seemed to me as a child that the advent of the new century changed everything as at the stroke of a magic wand. The city was gripped by the same financial frenzy as were the leading capitals of the world. Tall blocks of offices and flats sprang up overnight in an epidemic of speculative deals. All at once, brick giants reached into the sky from every street. And with them, Moscow, outstripping Petersburg, produced a new Russian art, the art of a big city, young, fresh and contemporary.

* * *

The College was affected by the same fever as the rest of the town. Its allocation from the Treasury was not sufficient for its upkeep; so private business men were asked to raise funds to cover the budget. It was decided to build and let many-storeyed blocks of flats on the College grounds, and glass-roofed premises suitable for exhibitions on the site of the garden. At the end of the 'nineties the sheds and outbuildings were pulled down, the garden was uprooted and deep trenches were dug in the ground. The trenches filled with water and in them, as in a pond, dead rats floated and frogs jumped and dived in off the banks. Our annexe was also scheduled for demolition.

That winter, two or three classrooms and lecture halls in the main building were converted into a new flat for us and we moved into it in 1901. As one of the apartments from which it had been carved out was round and another still more fancifully shaped, our dwelling for the next ten years had a bathroom and a box-room which together formed a crescent; the kitchen was oval and the dining-room had a semi-circle bitten out of it. There was always a muffled din coming from the passages and work-rooms outside, and from the end room Professor Chaplygin could be heard lecturing on heating methods to the architecture class next door.

For some years, while we were still in our old flat, I had been having lessons in preparation for going to school. Sometimes my mother taught me, some-times private teachers were engaged. For a while, when there was a plan to send me to the Peter and Paul High School,[4] I followed at home and in German all the subjects taught in its junior form.

Of the various teachers whom I gratefully remem-ber, I will mention the first, Yekaterina Ivanovna Baratynskaya, who wrote for children and translated children's stories from English. Starting from scratch, she showed me how to sit at table and hold a pen and taught me reading, writing and the begin-nings of arithmetic and French. She lived in a furnished room where I was taken for my lessons. The room was dark and stacked from floor to ceiling with books. It smelled of cleanliness, austerity, boiled milk and burned coffee. Lace curtains hung over the window; outside it, grubby, creamy-greyish snowflakes dropped like stitches. They distracted my attention. Yekaterina Ivanovna spoke to me in French and I replied at random. When the lesson was over she wiped her pen on the lining of her jacket, waited for me to be fetched and bundled me off.

In 1901 I entered the Second Form of the Fifth Moscow High School; after Vannovsky's reform [5] it had added natural science and other modern subjects to its curriculum but had kept its classical slant and continued to teach Greek.

* * *

In the spring of 1903 Father rented a *dacha* [6] in the country near to Maloyaroslavets on the Bryansk railway (now known as the Kiev Line). It turned out that Scriabin was our neighbour. We had not been on visiting terms with him until then.

The two houses stood at some distance from each other, beside a forest clearing on a hill. We arrived, as usually happens, early in the morning. The sun filtered into the rooms through the low branches which overhung our roof. Inside, bundles wrapped in sacking were cut open, and food, bed linen, frying-pans and pails unpacked. I escaped into the wood.

God Almighty, what that morning wood was filled with! The sunlight pierced it through and through from every side. Its moving shadows tilted its cap this way and that; and from its rising and falling branches came that always unexpected, always unfamiliar chirruping of birds which starts with loud, abrupt calls and, gradually dying down, repeats in its warm quick urgency the alternating lights and shadows of the trees running into the distance. And in exactly the same way as lights and shadows alternated and birds sang and fluttered from branch to branch, so fragments of the Third Symphony or *Divine Poem*, composed upon the piano in the neighbouring house, carried and resounded through the wood.

Lord, what music it was! Again and again the symphony tumbled into ruins like a shelled town and was built up and rose out of its rubble of destruction. Its theme, insanely elaborate, filled it to overflowing and was new—as the forest was new, breathing life and freshness, clothed in spring that morning in 1903—it wasn't 1803 remember! And just as in the forest there was not one leaf of coloured tinfoil or crinkled paper, so the symphony had no false depth in it, no solemn rhetoric, nothing to make it sound like Beethoven, or like Glinka, or like Ivan Ivanovich [7] or like Princess Maria Alexevna [8]; instead, its tragic power triumphantly thumbed its nose at everything respectably decrepit and majestically dull, and was insanely, mischievously daring, and free, frivolous and elemental as a fallen angel.

You would expect a man who composed such music to know what kind of a person he was and, in his hours of leisure, to be as tranquil and lucent as God resting from his labours on the seventh day; and such indeed he proved to be.

He and my father would often go for walks along the Warsaw Highway which cut across the countryside not far from our house. Sometimes I accompanied them. Scriabin liked to take a run and then to go on skipping along the road like a stone skimming the water, as if at any moment he might leave the ground and glide on air. In general, he had trained himself in various kinds of sublime lightness and unburdened movement verging on flight. Among such expressions of his character were his well-bred charm and his worldly manner of putting on a superficial air and avoiding serious subjects in society. All the more astonishing were his paradoxes in the course of these country walks.

He argued with my father about good and evil and life and art, he attacked Tolstoy and preached Nietzsche's superman and amoralism. They agreed only in their conception of the essence and problems of craftsmanship, in everything else they differed.

I was twelve at the time. Half their arguments were above my head. But Scriabin conquered me by the freshness of his mind. I worshipped him. I was always on his side though I hardly ever knew what he meant. Soon he left for Switzerland where he was to stay for six years.[9]

That autumn I had an accident which kept us in the country later than usual. Father was painting a picture, "To Night Pastures."[10] It was a sunset scene of girls from a nearby village, Bocharovo, riding at full tilt and driving horses to the water meadows at the bottom of our hill. One evening I joined them, but my horse ran away with me and, as it jumped a wide stream, I fell off and broke my leg. I was left with one leg shorter than the other and, as a result, was afterwards exempted from the army whenever there was a call-up.

Even before that summer I had strummed a little on the piano and had managed to put a few notes together of my own. Now, after my meeting with Scriabin, I longed passionately to compose. That autumn I began to study the theory of composition and devoted to it all my six remaining years at school; I worked with the admirable Engel, a musical critic and theoretician of that time, and later with Professor Glier.

No one had the slightest doubt of my vocation.

My future was settled. My parents were delighted with my choice of a career; music was to be my destiny—and every sort of ungrateful beastliness towards my elders, whose shoes I was unworthy to unlace, every form of mulish disobedience, neglect and eccentricity were forgiven me for its sake. Even when I was caught fiddling with some problem in fugue or counterpoint at school, a music book open on my desk in the middle of a lesson in mathematics or Greek, or stood gaping like a fool when I was asked a question, the whole class rose to my defence and the teachers overlooked my faults. And yet in spite of this I gave up music.

I gave it up at the very moment when I had reason to feel that I was doing well and congratulations were pouring in on me. My divinity had returned; Scriabin had come back from Switzerland bringing his latest compositions including *L'Extase*. His arrival was a triumph and the whole of Moscow was celebrating his return. At the height of the festivities I called on him and played my pieces. His reaction surpassed all my hopes. He heard me out, approved, encouraged me and gave me his blessing.

But no one knew of my secret trouble and, had I spoken of it, I would not have been believed. I was getting on as a composer but I played wretchedly and I read music like a child learning to spell. The discrepancy between my musical themes, new and difficult in themselves, and my lack of practical skill turned the natural gift which should have been a joy to me into a torment, and in the end I found it unendurable.

How could this have come about? There was something basically wrong, something which called for retribution, in my attitude. I had the adolescent arrogance, the nihilist conceit of the half-taught which despises whatever seems attainable, whatever can be "earned" by effort. I looked down on industry as uncreative, taking it upon myself to lay down the law on matters of which I knew nothing. "In real life," I thought, everything must be miraculous and pre-ordained, nothing must be planned, deliberate, willed.

This was the negative side of Scriabin's influence on me. I took him for my supreme authority, not realising that he alone could afford his own egocentricity, that his teaching was right only for him. I misunderstood him childishly, but the seeds of his opinions had fallen on fertile soil.

I had always had mystical and superstitious leanings and a hankering after providential signs. Almost as far back as the night of the concert I had started to believe in a heroic world which claimed my joyful service although it was a source of anguish. How often, as a child of six, seven or eight, had I been close to suicide!

I suspected that all sorts of mysteries and lies surrounded me. There was no absurdity which I did not believe. At moments, at the dawn of life, the only moment when such foolishness is thinkable, I imagined (perhaps because I could remember my nurse dressing me in my first smocks) that I remembered having been a girl, and that I could regain this earlier more pleasing, more fascinating personality, by pulling in my belt so tight that I almost fainted. At other times I thought that I was not my parents' son but a foundling whom they had adopted.

So too, in my misfortunes as a musician, devious and imaginary causes were involved—oracles and signs and omens. I lacked perfect pitch. This was quite unnecessary to me in my work, but the discovery was a grief and a humiliation and I took it as proof that my music was rejected by heaven or fate. I had not the courage to stand up to all these blows and I lost heart.

For six years I had lived for music. Now I tore it up and flung it from me as you throw away your dearest treasure. For a while, I went on improvising by habit but I was gradually losing my skill. Then I decided to make a clean break—I stopped

Boris Pasternak writing

Alexander Scriabin

playing the piano or going to concerts, and I avoided meeting musicians.

*   *   *

Scriabin's defence of the superman was an expression of his native Russian craving for the superlative. Indeed, it is not only true that music needs to be more than itself if it is to mean anything, but that everything in the world must surpass itself in order to be itself. There must be something limitless in a human being and in his activity for either to have definition and character.

In view of my broken ties with music and of my failure to keep up with its developments, the Scriabin of my memories—the Scriabin who used to be my daily bread—is the Scriabin of his middle period, roughly between his third and fifth sonatas.[11]

To me, the Promethean lightnings[12] of his last works are not the daily food of the soul but merely added evidence of his genius, and of such evidence I have no need since I took him on trust from the beginning.

Men who have died young, such as Andrey Bely and Khlebnikov, spent the last years of their lives looking for a new means of expression, dreaming of a new language, groping for its vowels, consonants and syllables.

I have never understood the need for this kind of research. I believe the most astonishing discoveries of all to have been made at moments when the sense of his work so possessed the artist that it left him no time to think and he was driven by his urgency to speak new words in the old language, without stopping to know if it was old or new.

That was how Chopin, using the old idiom of Mozart and Field, said so many new things in music that he seems to be its new beginning.

And this was how Scriabin, very early on in his career and using almost nothing but the methods of his forerunners, changed and renovated the climate of music. As early as the Etudes of the Eighth Opus and the Preludes of the Eleventh, his work was already wholly contemporary, it had an inner correspondence, in musical terms, to the surrounding world, to the way people thought, felt, lived, dressed and travelled in those days.

The melodies in these compositions start as tears start to your eyes, and flow as tears flow from the corners of your eyes, down your cheeks to the corners of your mouth. They flow along your bare nerves and heart, and your tears are not tears of sorrow but of astonishment because the way into your heart has been so perfectly discovered.

All at once, there breaks into the flow of melody

an answer to it, an objection in another, higher, feminine voice and in a simpler, conversational tone. The chance argument is resolved at once. But it leaves behind it the overwhelmingly disturbing note of that simplicity on which everything in art depends.

Art is full of generally accepted truths. But although their use is open to all, the well-known rules are hardly ever properly applied. A well-known truth needs special luck, the kind of luck that comes its way once in a century, to find its application. Scriabin was such a piece of luck. Just as Dostoyevsky was more than a mere novelist and Blok more than a mere poet, Scriabin was more than merely a composer—he is an everlasting reason for rejoicing and congratulation, a feast, a celebration in the history of Russian culture.

CHAPTER THREE

The Nineteen Hundreds

IN answer to the student demonstrations which followed the Manifesto of 17th October,[1] the rabble of Okhotny Ryad [2] looted the University and the Higher Technical Schools. The College was also threatened. By the Director's orders, piles of stones were kept on the landings of the main staircase and lengths of hose connected with the taps for use against possible raiders.

Every now and then, a crowd marching down our street turned aside and entered the building. Classrooms were occupied, meetings were held in the Assembly Hall, and from the balcony speakers addressed those who had remained in the street below. The College students formed their own militant organisations and our own home guard was on duty at night.

Among my father's papers is a drawing of a girl speaking from the balcony; she is wounded and supporting herself against a pillar; dragoons are charging the crowd and shooting at her.

At the end of 1905, at the height of the general strike [3], Gorky came back to Moscow. The nights were frosty; the pitch-black city was lit by bonfires. Stray bullets whistled down the empty streets, and mounted patrols charged with soundless fury over the untrodden snow.

My father saw Gorky several times in connection with the various new satirical papers, such as *The Scourge* and *The Bugaboo* [4] to whose editorial offices Gorky would invite him.

It was about that time, I think—though it may have been later, when we had returned to Moscow after a year's stay in Berlin [5]—that I came across a poem by Blok. I no longer remember what it was—perhaps the "Pussywillows" or something from *Childhood* [6] dedicated to Olenina d'Alheim, or something about the town and the revolution—but I remember my impression of it so distinctly that I am able to revive and to describe it now.

* * *

What do we usually mean by "literature"? A world of rhetoric, triteness, rounded phrases and respectable names, of people who have looked at life when they were young but who, once they have achieved fame, confine themselves to abstractions, to rehashing and to cautious common sense. Whenever, in this kingdom in which artificiality is so established that it goes unnoticed, anyone opens his mouth not out of a taste for verbal elegance but because he knows a thing and wants to say it, the result is an upheaval, as if the doors had been flung open and let in the noises of the street; not as if the speaker were reporting on events in town but as if the town itself were giving notice of its presence through his lips. This happened in the case of Blok; so great was the effective power of his lonely, childlike, uncorrupted speech.

You looked at any one of his poems: it contained a piece of news. It seemed as if the piece of news had settled on the page of its own accord without anyone's permission, as if the poem had not been written down by anyone. What you saw was not a poem about wind and puddles and stars and street lamps, but the lamp-lit puddles rippling, wind-chased over the surface of the paper and leaving on it their strong, damp, disturbing trace.

* * *

Blok was part of my youth, as of the youth of others of my generation (I will speak of them later). He had all the qualities which go to make a great poet—

passion, gentleness, dedicated insight, his own conception of the world, his own gift of transforming everything he touched, his own reserved, restrained, self-effacing destiny. Of all these qualities and many others besides, I will mention only one aspect—I found it the most striking and it therefore seemed to me predominant in him: his swiftness, his wandering yet attentive glance, the quickness of his observations.

> A light swung in the window.
> Alone in the half-dark,
> A harlequin whispered
> With the darkness at the doorway
>
> The sweeping blizzard
> Swings up the streets:
> A hand reaches out to me
> Somebody smiles.
>
> A teasing light waves,
> Blacks out like a face on a winter night
> When the silhouette of a shadow
> Slips through the porch.[7]

Adjectives without a noun, predicates without a subject, alarm, excitement, hide-and-seek, abruptness, whisking shadows—how well this style accorded with the spirit of the time, itself secretive, hermetic, underground, only just out of the cellars and still using the language of conspiracy, the spirit of a time and of a tale in which the chief character was the town and the street was the chief event.

These are the qualities which permeate the being of Blok, this is the essential and predominating Blok—the Blok of the second volume of the Alkonost edition, the author of *The Terrible World*, *The Last Day*, *Fraud*, *Story*, *Legend*, *Meeting*, *Stranger*, and the poems " In mist above the sparkling dew", " In pubs, alleys and lanes", and " A girl sang in the choir ". [8]

Drawn by his perceptiveness, reality whirls into his poems like a stream of air. This is true of everything in his poetry, down to its apparent mysticism and " theology", which are not a form of metaphysical brooding but a scattering throughout his verse of torn fragments of the daily reality of church-going life—passages from litanies, communion prayers, burial psalms, versicles which he knew by heart through having heard them hundreds of times in church.

The sum, the heart, the bearer of all this reality was the city, the Petersburg of his poems—for Petersburg was the real hero of his story, the subject of his biography.

Of all the Petersburgs conceived by artists of our time, his is the most real. It exists equally and indistinguishably in imagination and in life; it is full of the prose of its daily round, the prose which communicates drama and unrest to poetry, and the language spoken in its streets is the current language of colloquial conversation by which poetic language is refreshed.

And yet the features of this portrait of a town are drawn by so sensitive a hand and are so spiritualised, that the whole of it is also the absorbing image of a most remarkable inner world.

* * *

I had been lucky enough to get to know many of the older poets who lived in Moscow [9] but I was only introduced to Blok when he came to Moscow for the last time.[10] It was on the night of a poetry reading at the Polytechnical Museum: I met him on the stairs or on the landing outside the lecture hall. He was very friendly; he said that he had heard nothing but good of me and would like to know me, but that he was feeling ill that evening and would have to put off seeing me until he was better.

That evening he was to read poetry in three different places—at the Polytechnic, at the Press Club, and at the Dante Society where an enthusiastic audience of his followers was awaiting him to hear his " Italian Poems ".

Mayakovsky whom I met at the Polytechnic told me that a plot had been cooked up at the Press Club and that, under the pretext of independent criticism, Blok was to be received with catcalls, whistles and abuse. Mayakovsky suggested that we should go there and try to prevent this infamy.

We set off immediately, but, since we went on foot, while Blok, as soon as he had finished at the Polytechnic, was taken by car, it was all over by the time we reached the club in the Nikitsky Boulevard. Blok had already left for the Dante Society. The row had been as bad as we had feared. After the reading, insults had been showered on him; he was even told to his face that he was a " back number " and a " living corpse "; with all of this he quietly agreed. And all of this was said to him a few months before his death.[11]

* * *

In those years of our first experiments only two poets of our generation possessed the mastery of an accomplished and mature poetic style: they were Aseyev and Tsvetayeva. As for the rest of us, our boasted originality, including mine, came from our complete and helpless inarticulateness, which did not prevent us from writing, publishing and translating verse. Of all the depressing and incompetent pieces I wrote at that time the most horrible were my translations of Ben Jonson's *Alchemist* and of Goethe's *Mysteries.*[12] Blok reviewed my version of *Mysteries* for the publishers of *World Literature* and the review was afterwards included with others in the last volume of his Collected Works. Its crushingly contemptuous tone was just and well deserved. But I have run ahead of my story and must go back to where I left it, far back in the early nineteen hundreds.

* * *

When I was in my third or fourth form at school, I spent the Christmas holidays in Petersburg.[13] My uncle, who was head of the Petersburg goods station on the Nikolayevsky Line, gave me a warrant and I travelled up by myself by train. All day long I wandered about the streets of the immortal city, as if my eyes and feet were devouring some work of genius in stone; I spent my evenings at Kommissarzhevskaya's Theatre.[14] I was intoxicated by the latest books; I raved about Andrey Bely, Hamsun, Przybyszewski.

An even wider, more genuine experience of travelling was our journey to Berlin where we all went in 1906. For the first time in my life I was abroad.

Everything was unusual, different from what it

was at home. It was less like living than like dreaming, or like taking part in some improvisation on the stage, some entertainment without rules, which no one had a duty to take part in or attend. There was nobody you knew, nobody to lay down the law to you—doors flapping open and shut in an endless row along the lane of carriages—each compartment with its separate door. Four tracks curving along a circular viaduct overlooking the gigantic city, high above its streets, canals, racing stables and back yards. Trains chasing and overtaking one another, running side by side and separating. Street lights dividing, intersecting under railway bridges; lights in first and second storey windows, level with the tracks; jewelled clusters of pin-point illumination on slot machines in station restaurants (the slot machines threw out cigars, chocolates and sugared almonds). I was soon familiar with Berlin, loafing about in its countless streets and in its endless park, breathing its mixture of gas, train smoke and beer fumes, talking German with a fake *Berliner* accent and listening to Wagner.

Berlin was full of Russians. The composer Rebikov played his " Christmas Tree " for his friends and explained that there were three periods in music: bestial until Beethoven, human between Beethoven and Rebikov, and the music of the future.

Gorky too was in Berlin.[15] My father made a drawing of him. Andreyeva disliked it: the cheek-bones were too prominent so that the face looked angular. She said: " You haven't understood him. He is Gothic." That was how they spoke in those days.

* * *

It must have been soon after our return to Moscow that another great contemporary lyric poet came into my life; this was the German, Rainer Maria Rilke,[16] who was hardly known in those days but who is now recognised by the whole world.

In 1900 he had been to see Tolstoy at Yasnaya Polyana. He had spent one summer with the peasant poet Drozhzin in the country, at Zavidovo, near Klin, and he knew and corresponded with my father.

In those far-off days when his early poems were being published, he sent my father copies of his books inscribed with friendly dedications. Two such books happened to fall into my hands that winter, long after they had arrived. They shook me by the same insistent, unconditional gravity, the same directness in the use of language as had first astonished me in Blok.

* * *

In Russia Rilke is unknown. The few translations of him have been unsuccessful. The translators are not to blame. They are used to conveying meaning but not tone, and in Rilke tone is everything.

I had no idea of his reputation abroad until one day in 1913, when Verhaeren, who was in Moscow, was sitting for his portrait. My father asked me, as he did sometimes, to amuse his model so that his expression should not grow set and lifeless. In this way I had had to entertain the historian Klyuchevsky. Now it was Verhaeren. Needless to say I was a great admirer of his work and spoke to him about it; then I asked him diffidently if he had ever heard of Rilke. I could not imagine that he actually knew him. Verhaeren was transfigured. My father could not have asked for anything better than the change in his expression at the mere sound of Rilke's name. " He is the best poet in Europe," said Verhaeren, " and my beloved spiritual brother."

Unlike Blok, who regarded prose as the source of poetry but who did not integrate it in his own writing, Rilke looked on the descriptive and psychological discoveries of the novelists of his time (Tolstoy, Flaubert, Proust and the Scandinavians) as intimately linked with his own poetic language and style.

However, I could go on describing and analysing

him for ever without giving any clear impression of his work unless I gave an example.[17]

* * *

It was in about 1907 that a crop of new publishers sprang up like mushrooms, modern compositions were performed at many concerts, and art exhibitions opened one after another—" The World of Art ", " The Golden Fleece ", " The Knave of Diamonds ", " The Donkey's Tail ", " The Blue Rose ".[18] Among the many Russian names—Somov, Sapunov, Sudeykin, Krymov, Laryonov, Goncharova—flickered the names of Frenchmen—Bonnard, Vuillard. Pictures by Matisse and sculptures by Rodin arrived from Paris and could be seen at The Golden Fleece, in darkly curtained halls which smelled of mould like hot-houses, so crowded were they with pots of hyacinths. Many young people joined the new artistic movements.

An old wooden house still stood in the courtyard of one of the new blocks of flats in Razgulyay Square. The owner lived in it; he was a general. On the top floor the General's son, the poet and painter Julian Anisimov, gathered round him a circle of young people who shared his interests. He had a weak chest and spent the winter abroad, but on fine evenings in spring and autumn he gave parties at which there were reading, music, sketching, arguments, and tea laced with rum. There I met a great many people.

The host, a most gifted being, a man of excellent taste, well read and cultivated, speaking several languages as fluently as Russian, was the embodiment of that poetic quality which gives charm to the amateur but is difficult to combine with a strong creative personality or the character of a master craftsman. We had many tastes and interests in common. I liked him very much.

It was at Anisimov's that I met Sergey Durylin, who has since died; at that time he was writing under the pseudonym of Sergey Rayevsky. In his kindness he managed to see something worthy of attention in my first experiments and it was under his influence that I was finally won over from music to writing. He lived in great poverty, keeping his mother and his aunt by giving lessons, and his ardent integrity and fanatical convictions recalled the figure of Belinsky as it is handed down to us by legend.

It was also at Anisimov's that Loks, whom I already knew—he was my fellow student at the University—first made me read Innokenty Annensky, a remarkable poet until then unknown to me, be-

Boris Pasternak as a young man

Leonid Pasternak

tween whose work and my scribblings Loks had established an imaginary kinship.

Our circle had a name. It had been christened " Serdarda "; none of us knew what this meant. It was understood that Arkady Guryev, a poet and singer and a member of the circle, had once heard it on the Volga. He heard it at night, in the confusion which inevitably happens when two boats arrive almost simultaneously at a landing stage: the two are lashed side by side, and the passengers of the second arrival go ashore with their luggage through the bowels of the first, and get entangled with its passengers and all their things.

Guryev came from Saratov. He had a deep, gentle, powerful voice and the art of bringing out every tonal and dramatic subtlety of anything he sang. Like most rough diamonds,[19] he astonished one as much by his incessant fooling as by the depth and genuineness which showed occasionally through his affectation. His verse was well above the average, and our delight in it foreshadowed our delight in Mayakovsky's immoderate sincerity and in Yesenin's clean-out images, conveyed in all their freshness to the reader. An accomplished operatic singer and dramatic artist, he was that very essence of the born actor which Ostrovsky has portrayed so often.

He had a head as round as an onion with a big forehead, a nose that hardly showed at all and a bald patch which promised to spread from brow to nape. He was all movement, all expression. He never gestured with his hands, but as he stood arguing or reciting his whole body moved, acted, spoke. Torso thrown back, head sideways, legs wide apart, he looked as if he had been struck motionless in the middle of a Russian dance. When he was drunk he would start believing his own nonsense. At the end of a turn he would pretend that his foot was stuck to the floor and assure us that the devil had him by the heel.

To the Serdarda came poets and painters, Krasin who had set Blok's " Pussywillows " to music; Bobrov whose early poems were published with mine and whose appearance in Razgulyay was preceded by his reputation as a newly-hatched Russian Rimbaud; Kozhebatkin, the editor of *Musaget* [20]; and, when he was in Moscow, Sergey Makovsky, the editor of *Apollo*.

I joined the Serdarda on the strength of my reputation as a musician; as the guests arrived I improvised musical sketches of each of them.

The short spring night was soon over. The cold morning breathed through the open windows. Its breath lifted the hems of the curtains, stirred the flame of the guttering candles and rustled the papers scattered on the table. We all yawned—host, guests, the empty distance, the grey sky, the rooms, the stairs. Finally we went home along the wide streets which seemed longer through being empty, overtaking as we went the procession of rattling cesspool carts. "Centaurs," one of us would say in the idiom of the time.

*   *   *

A sort of school grew up around the *Musaget.* Writers and critics [21] lectured to eager young people on poetic rhythm, the history of German romanticism, Russian lyric poetry, the æsthetics of Goethe and Richard Wagner; Baudelaire and the French symbolists, and pre-Socratic Greek philosophy.

The heart and soul of all this activity was Andrey Bely, the unchallenged leader of the movement. He was a first-rate poet and even more remarkable as the prose-writer of the *Symphonies* and of the two novels *The Silver Dove* and *Petersburg*, which transformed pre-revolutionary Russian taste and were the starting point of Soviet prose.

Bely had all the marks of genius—it was a genius which, unharnessed by daily difficulties, family life or the incomprehension of his friends, raced in a vacuum and had turned from a creative power into a barren and destructive force. This failing which arose from an excess of inspiration did not lower him in our eyes but gained our sympathy and added to his attraction a note of suffering.

He gave a practical course on Russian iambic verse and in discussion with his students used statistics to explain its rhythmic figures and variations. I took no part in this discussion group for I believed then, as I still do now, that verbal music is not a matter of acoustics or of harmonising vowels and consonants as such, but of relating sound to meaning.

One of the places where the young enthusiasts of the *Musaget* occasionally gathered was the studio of the sculptor Krakht in the Presnya district.

Half-way up the walls there was a gallery which Krakht used as his bedroom; below it on the floor, white among the decorative plants and draping ivy, were clay masks, casts of antique fragments and his own works.

One evening in the late autumn I went to Krakht's to read a paper on " Symbolism and Immortality ". Part of the audience sat on the floor, the rest lay on the floor of the gallery hanging their heads over the edge.

My thesis was based on the idea that our impressions are subjective, that there is a difference between the sounds and colours we perceive and the corresponding sound and light vibrations which exist objectively in the world around us. I developed the idea that these subjective impressions and the capacity to receive them are not an attribute of the separate individual but are suprapersonal and racial, the common property of the world of man, of the human race. I assumed that every human being leaves behind him when he dies his own share of this undying, racial subjectivity—the share contained in him in his lifetime and which enabled him to take part in human history. My purpose was to suggest that in this ultimate, subjective and yet universal area of the soul, art finds its everlasting field of action and its main content; and that although the artist is of course mortal like everyone else, the joy of living experienced by him is immortal and can be felt by others through his work, centuries after his death, in a form approximating to that of his original, intimately personal experience.

The paper was called "Symbolism and Immortality" because it maintained that, in the sense in which it is possible to speak of symbols in algebra, all art is in essence conventional and symbolic.

The audience was interested and the discussion which followed went on late into the night. When I got home I heard that Tolstoy, who had left his home at Yasnaya Polyana and collapsed at the railway station of Astapovo, had died.[22] Father had been summoned to Astapovo by telegram. We went off at once to catch the night train from Paveletsky Station.

* * *

In those days the difference between town and country was greater than it is now, the transition as you left town was more abrupt. From early morning onwards, the same endless view of ploughed or fallow land, hardly varied by scattered villages, filled the carriage window: this was the thousand mile expanse of Russian peasant countryside which laboured for and fed the small urban Russia of that time. The fields were already silvered by the first frosts and were still framed along their boundaries by the gold remaining on the birch trees; and these modest ornaments of hoar-frost silver and birch-tree gold lay upon the land like the gold and silver-leaf illumination of its holy and meek antiquity.

The land resting, ploughed or fallow, flickered outside the window, knowing nothing of the death, nearby, of the last of her giants. A man fit by birth to be her tsar and the sophistication of whose mind, surfeited by all the refinements of the world, could have made him the favourite among all favourites, the lordling among lordlings, but who, for love of her and out of scrupulous concern for her, had instead followed the plough, dressed and belted like a peasant.

*   *   *

Those who had been taking leave of Tolstoy's body had probably been asked to wait outside while a drawing of him and then a death mask were being made (Merkurov had brought a caster). We came into an empty room. Then Sofya Andreyevna [23] rose and came forward hurriedly from the far corner; she clutched my father's hands and spoke feverishly through her tears: "Oh, what I have been through, Leonid Osipovich! You know how much I loved him," and she went on to tell Father how, when Tolstoy left home, she had tried to drown herself and was dragged half dead out of the lake.

Tolstoy's presence filled the room like a mountain—say like Elbrus—or like a storm cloud the size of half a sky. And Tolstoy's widow was as much a part of it as a great cliff taken from the mountain or as lightning flashing from the cloud. But she did not know that she had the right of cliffs and lightning to be silent and unaccountable in her acts; that she need not enter into argument with the Tolstoyans who had less in common with Tolstoy than anyone in the world; that she had only to ignore their pigmy challenge.[24]

So she justified herself and called upon my father to bear witness that her devotion to her husband and her understanding of his mind were greater than her rivals', and that she could have taken better care of him than they did. God, I thought, how can anyone—let alone Tolstoy's wife—be reduced to this!

It really is strange! A modern critic with an up-to-date outlook, who condemns duelling in general as an antiquated custom, has published an enormous work on Pushkin's duel and his death.[25] Poor Pushkin! Why didn't he marry Shchegolev and modern Pushkinology? Then everything would have been in order. He would still be alive to-day, and he would have written several sequels to *Evgeny Onegin* and five *Poltavas* instead of only one. My own feeling has always been that I would not understand a word of Pushkin if I admitted for a moment that our understanding of him meant more to him than did his wife.[26]

* * *

But what there was in the far corner of the room was not a mountain but a wrinkled little old man, one of the dozens of old men invented by Tolstoy and scattered through his books. The place bristled with fir saplings which stood round the bed, their outlines sharpened by the setting sun. Four slanting sheaves of light reached across the room and threw over the corner where the body lay the sign of the big shadow of the crosspiece of the window and the small, childish crosses of the shadows of the firs.

That day the station of Astapovo had turned into the braying camp of the world Press. Trade was brisk at the station restaurant. Waiters were run off their feet, hardly able to keep up with orders and galloping with plates of underdone beef steaks. Beer flowed like a river.

Waiting at the station were Tolstoy's sons Ilya and Andrey. Sergey was on the train which came to fetch Tolstoy's body and take it to Yasnaya Polyana.

Students and young people, singing " Eternal Memory ", bore the coffin across the small station yard, the garden and the platform to the waiting train and put it in the guard's van. The mourners who crowded on the platform bared their heads, and to the sound of renewed singing the train moved slowly in the direction of Tula.

It was somehow natural that Tolstoy should have found his rest and found it by the wayside like a pilgrim, close to one of Russia's railways on which his heroes and heroines continued to fly past and round and round, unaware, as they glanced out of the carriage window and caught sight of the small station, that here the eyes which had observed them and immortalised them had closed for ever.

* * *

If every writer were to be described by only one of his outstanding qualities—as we might speak of the passionate quality of Lermontov, of Tyutchev's fecundity of thought, of Chekhov's poetry, of Gogol's dazzling brilliance, or of the power of Dostoyevsky's imagination—what should we then say of Tolstoy?

Tolstoy was a moralist, a leveller, a preacher of a system of justice applicable to every human being without exception and in equal measure; yet the most outstanding of his qualities was his originality—an originality which goes to the point of paradox.

Throughout his life he could always look at an event and see the whole of it, in the isolated, self-contained finality of its moment, as a vivid and exhaustive sketch—see it as the rest of us can only see on rare occasions, in childhood, or at a crest of happiness which renews the world, or in the joy of some great spiritual victory.

To have this vision the eye needs to be directed by passion. It is the flaring up of passion that illuminates the object and intensifies its visibility.

Such a passion—the passion of creative contemplation—Tolstoy bore incessantly within himself. And it was in its light that he could see each thing in its primordial freshness, in a new way and as though for the first time. The genuineness of his vision is so outside our normal habits that it may strike us as strange. But he did not look for this strangeness, he did not pursue it as an aim, still less did he use it as a literary device.

CHAPTER FOUR

Eve of the First World War

I SPENT the spring and summer of 1912 abroad. Our summer vacations coincide with the summer term in Western universities; I spent it at the ancient University of Marburg.

It was there that Lomonosov had studied under the great mathematician and philosopher Christian Wolff; and there, a century and a half earlier, Giordano Bruno had broken his return journey to Rome to read a paper on his new system of astronomy, before going home—and to his death at the stake.

Marburg was a small and picturesque medieval town. In those days it had a population of twenty-nine thousand; half were students. Moulded into the contours of a hill where the stone of its houses, churches, university and castle had been quarried, it was sunk deep in gardens as dark as night.

At the end of the term I had a few pennies left of the sum provided for my studies and my keep in

Germany; I used them to go on to Italy. I saw Venice, brick rose and aquamarine like the transparent pebbles on a beach, and Florence, dark, beautiful, cooped up, snatched bodily out of Dante; I ran out of money before I could visit Rome.[1]

In the following year I took my degree at the University of Moscow. Mansurov, a young historian who had stayed on at the University as a postgraduate, lent me a mass of books which he had used in preparing for his own examinations the year before. There was more than enough in his professorial library to satisfy the examiners—not only general text books but detailed reference works on classical antiquities and monographs on special subjects. I could hardly get all this wealth into a cab when I took it home.

Mansurov had two friends who were also his kinsmen, young Nikolay Trubetskoy and Dmitry Samarin. I had known them at school where they came to sit for their end of year examinations although they worked the rest of the time at home.

There were two older Trubetskoys teaching at the university; Nikolay's father held the Chair of general theory of Law, while his uncle, a well-known philospher, was the Rector. Both of them remarkably stout, they lumbered on to the dais like elephants dressed up in waistless coats, and delivered their splendid lectures in imploring accents and in droning, whining voices with an aristocratic lisp.[2]

The three young people had a family look. Tall, gifted youths, with eyebrows joined together in a single line and voices as resounding as their names, they dropped in at the university as an inseparable trio.

The Marburg philosophical school[3] was greatly honoured in their circle. Trubetskoy's uncle wrote about it and encouraged his most promising students to attend its courses. Samarin who had been to them before me was at home in Marburg and a Marburg patriot, and it was on his advice that I went there myself.

Samarin came from a famous Slavophil family[4]; they had a property near Moscow, on which the Writers' Settlement of Peredelkino[5] and the Peredelkino Tuberculosis Sanatorium for children stand to-day.

Philosophy, dialectics and Hegelian scholarship were in Samarin's blood as a hereditary gift. He was disorderly, absent-minded and almost certainly a little mad. The eccentricities which startled his friends when the mood was on him made him impossible to live with. He was always quarrelling with his relations and they could not be blamed for falling out with him.

At the beginning of the NEP [6] Samarin, dishevelled, stripped of sophistication and full of all-forgiving understanding, came back to Moscow from Siberia where the Civil War had tossed him to and fro for a long time. He was swollen with hunger and covered with lice from his journey. He caught typhus and died towards the end of the epidemic.

The fate of Mansurov is unknown to me. The philologist, Nikolay Trubetskoy, achieved a world-wide reputation and has died recently in Vienna.

* * *

After my finals I spent the summer [7] at my parents' *dacha* in Molodi, near the station of Stolbovaya on the Moscow-Kursk railway.

According to tradition, Cossacks who were part of our retreating army had used the house as a snipers' nest against the forward units of Napoleon. Their graves, sunk and overgrown, could still be seen in the graveyard at the far end of the park.

The rooms were narrow in proportion to their height and had tall windows. At night the oil-lamp threw gigantic shadows on the ceiling and the dark, Bordeaux-coloured walls.

At the bottom of the park there was a narrow winding stream with many deep eddies and, leaning over it almost upside down, an old birch tree, half up-rooted but still growing.

The thick green tangle of its branches hanging in mid-air above the water made a summer-house; you could lie or sit in it in comfort. I made it my work-room.

I read Tyutchev and, for the first time in my life, wrote poetry not as a rare exception but regularly, every day, as people paint or compose music.

Perched in my tree, I wrote all the poems for my first book in those two or three summer months.

With stupid pretentiousness, I called the book *Twin in the Clouds*; this was in imitation of the cosmological obscurities of the book-titles of the symbolists and of the imprints of their publishers.

To write these poems—to scribble, to scratch out and to restore the vanished lines—this was my need and my joy, a joy which nothing else could give me and which moved me to tears.

I did my best to avoid poetic coquetry.[8] I felt no need to thunder my verses from a platform and make the hair rise on the heads of intellectuals with indignation at their " barbarism " and " vulgarity "; nor to read them to a closed circle of a chosen few who would congratulate me on my " integrity ", nor to make highbrow ladies swoon with rapture at their discreet refinement. Nor was I trying to achieve a

Leo Tolstoy

Maxim Gorky

song or dance-tune rhythm, so marked and jolly that it sets the arms and legs of hearers jigging almost without help from words. I was not expressing or reflecting or portraying or reacting against anything.

It was only later, when an attempt was made to establish a resemblance between Mayakovsky and myself, that I was credited with a gift for tonal and rhetorical effects. This is quite untrue—I have no more of this gift than anyone who uses words.

On the contrary, my concern has always been for meaning, and my dream that every poem should have content in itself—a new thought or a new image. And that the whole of it with all its individual character should be engraved so deeply into the book that it should speak from it with all the silence and with all the colours of its colourless black print.

Thus I wrote a poem called "Venice", and another called "The Railway Station". What I saw before me as I was writing was the town standing on the water, the figures-of-eight and circles of its reflections drifting, multiplying, swelling like a biscuit soaked in tea. Or the distance of the railway station, where the tracks and platforms end in clouds and smoke and the trains vanish, and the skyline of departure ends the history of situations—

meetings and farewells and events before and after them.

I was concerned neither with myself nor with my readers nor with the theory of art. All I cared about was that one poem should contain the town of Venice, and the other the Brest (now called the Byelorussian-Baltic) railway station.

Bobrov liked the lines, " The shifts of trains and of misfortunes would unfold the West."[9] He and Aseyev with several beginners like myself had started a small publishing firm on a co-operative basis. Bobrov who had a knowledge of typography from having worked for *Russian Archive*[10] produced his own books and ours. He published my *Twin* with a friendly introduction by Aseyev.

The wife of the poet Baltrushaytis told me that it was immature and that some day I would be sorry I had brought it out. I have indeed often regretted it.[11]

* * *

I was staying with the Baltrushaytis family in the hot summer of '14, the summer of the drought and of the total eclipse of the sun. This was on a big estate on the Oka[12] near the town of Alexia. I gave lessons to his son and worked on a translation of Kleist's comedy, *The Broken Jug;* it had been commissioned by the newly founded Studio Theatre [13] to which Baltrushaytis acted as literary adviser.

Nearby, at Tarusa, Balmont was translating Kalidasa's *Shakuntala* for the same Studio Theatre, and several other people connected with the arts lived on the estate—the poet Vyacheslav Ivanov, the painter Ulyanov and the wife of the writer Muratov.

In July I went to Moscow for my call-up, but was exempted because my riding accident as a child had left me with one leg shorter than the other.

One evening soon after my return to the country there was a curious happening on the Oka. For a long time we heard some kind of regimental music —marching songs and polkas—drifting slowly towards us down the river, but we could see nothing but the low mist clinging to the reeds. Then a small steam tug nosed its way round a promontory with three barges in tow. The people on the boat must have caught sight of the house on the hill and decided to land, for the tug turned, cut across the stream and pulled the barges over to our bank. We saw then that there were soldiers on them—a large contingent of Grenadiers. The men came ashore and lit campfires at the bottom of the hill. The officers were asked up to the house to dine and spend the night. Next morning they all sailed away. This was one of the incidents of the advance mobilisation. A few days later the war broke out.

* * *

After this I spent almost a year—two stretches with several breaks—as tutor to the son of a rich merchant, Morritz Philipp [14]; my pupil, Walter, was a charming and affectionate boy.

In the summer, when there were anti-German demonstrations and raiders broke into the premises of several big German firms such as Einem's and Ferrein's,[15] Philipp's office and his private house were wrecked and looted.

The raids were carried out according to plan and with the knowledge of the police. Only the property of the employers was supposed to suffer, that of the people they employed was left untouched. Most of my belongings, including all my clothes, were spared, but in the confusion my books and manuscripts got into the general chaos and were destroyed.

Later, I lost many of my manuscripts in more peaceful circumstances. I dislike my style before 1940, just as I quarrel with half of Mayakovsky's writings and with some of Yesenin's. I dislike the disintegrating forms, the impoverished thought and the littered and uneven language of those days. I have no regrets for the faulty works I lost. For quite a different reason I do not regret the loss of my successful writings either.

It is more important in life to lose than to acquire. Unless the seed dies it bears no fruit. One must live tirelessly, looking to the future, and drawing upon those reserves of life which are created not only by remembrance but also by forgetting.

At various times and for various reasons I have lost my paper on "Symbolism and Immortality", several articles written in my futuristic period, a fairytale for children in prose, two poems, a note-book of verse which should have come between *Above the Barriers* and *My Sister, Life*, several foolscap note-books containing the rough draft of a novel (except for the first chapter which I revised and published as a story, *The Childhood of Luvers*) and the translation of one whole tragedy from Swinburne's trilogy on Mary Stuart.

The Philipps moved from their burned and looted house into a furnished flat. I went with them. I remember my room. The rays of the setting autumn sun furrowed the room and the book of which I turned the pages. The evening was reflected as a pale pink bloom upon the pages of the book. And evening, in another of its aspects, was the heart, the matter of the poems it contained. I envied the simplicity of the author's means and the reality which they had netted. It was one of Akhmatova's early works, probably her *Plantain*.[16]

* * *

In the intervals of coaching Walter, I stayed in the Urals and in the Kama district. I spent a winter in Vsevolodo-Vilva, north of Perm, once visited by Chekhov and by Levitan, according to the memoirs of A. N. Tikhonov who describes it. Another winter I spent in the Tikhy Mountains working in the Ushkovs' chemical factory near the Kama.[17]

For some time I was responsible for examining the cases of men of military age whose work at the factory was a reserved occupation, and I released whole townships of potential recruits.

In winter the Urals factories kept in touch with the outside world by prehistoric methods of communication. The mail was carried from Kazan, a distance of two hundred miles,[18] by troika as in the days of the Captain's daughter.[19] I once made this journey.

In March 1917 the news of the outbreak of the revolution in Petersburg reached the factory and I went to Moscow.

My first stop was to be at the Izhevsk works[20] where I had to pick up the engineer Zvarsky, a remarkable man, to put myself under his orders and continue the journey with him.

All night and part of the next day we raced down from the Tikhy Mountains in a small covered wagon on sleighs. Muffled in three sheepskins and smothered in hay, I rolled helplessly from side to side at the bottom of the wagon like a sack. I dozed, slept and woke up, opened and closed my eyes.

I could see the forest road and the stars in the frosty night. Tall snowdrifts humped the narrow track like hills. Often, the wagon caught the lower branches of the overhanging pines, scattering their snow and scratching along them as it rustled noisily underneath. The starlight was reflected in the whiteness of the sheet of snow and lit the way. The shining pall of snow was frightening in the deep thickness of the woods, as if a burning candle had been set into the forest.

The three horses raced in single file, harnessed head to tail, now one now another swerving out of line; the coachman kept pulling them in, and when the wagon keeled over he jumped out and ran alongside, propping it with his shoulder to keep it from overturning.

Again I slept, losing consciousness of time, and was aroused suddenly by a jolt and the cessation of movement.

The coaching station in the forest was like a camp of robbers in a fairytale. A light glimmered in a hut. A clock ticked and a samovar simmered. While the coachman who had brought the wagon undid his things and warmed himself, talking with the woman who was getting him supper in a quiet, night-time voice, not to disturb whoever was asleep the other side of the partition, the new coachman wiped his lips and his moustache, buttoned up his coat and went out into the frost to harness the new troika.

And again the horses raced, the sleigh whistled over the snow and I dozed and slept. Then, the next day, there were factory chimneys in the distance, the limitless snow desert of a vast frozen river, and a railway track.

* * *

Bobrov treated me with undeserved warmth. He watched ceaselessly over my integrity as a futurist and kept me from all harmful influences. By these he understood the sympathy of my elders. Lest their kindness should lead me into academic ways, he rushed in the moment he saw the least sign of anyone taking an interest in me and obliged me, by whatever means, to break off the dangerous connection he had noted. Thanks to him I was always breaking with someone.

I liked Julian Anisimov and his wife Vera Stanevich. Bobrov dragged me into his quarrel with them and I lost their friendship.

Vyacheslav Ivanov wrote a touching dedication in the copy which he gave me of his book. Bobrov made fun of it in Bryusov's circle, in such a way that I seemed to have put him up to it. Next time he saw me, Vyacheslav Ivanov cut me dead.

A periodical, *The Contemporary*,[21] printed my translation of Kleist's comedy, *The Broken Jug*. My work was immature and dull. I ought to have been humbly grateful to the periodical for printing it, and still more grateful to the unknown editor who had revised it, greatly to its benefit.

But modesty, gratitude, sense of truth, were not in currency among the young artistic circles of the left; such feelings were considered mawkish. The proper thing was to be insolent and strut about sticking one's nose up in the air, and although it sickened me, I tagged along not to be left behind.

Something went wrong with the proofs of my translation. I got them late and compositors' notes somehow came to be included in the text.

Bobrov, to do him justice, had no idea of what was going on and, on this occasion, really did not know what he was doing. He said the whole thing was a disgrace—both the printer's errors and the unasked-for corrections of the style of the manuscript: I couldn't possibly let it pass. I must complain to Gorky; Bobrov had heard that he was somehow unofficially connected with the magazine. I followed his advice. Instead of thanking the board of *The Contemporary* I wrote Gorky an idiotic letter, full of ignorance, conceit and affectation, complaining of what in fact had been the kindness and consideration they had shown me. Years passed, and I discovered that I had complained to Gorky about Gorky. The manuscript had been printed on his instructions and it was he who had corrected it with his own hand.

Even my first meeting with Mayakovsky was the result of an encounter between two rival futurist groups; he belonged to one and I to the other. The organisers had counted on a row, but the difficulty was that our mutual understanding became obvious from our first words.

* * *

I will not speak of my relations with Mayakovsky at length.[22] Our friendship was never close. His account of it has been exaggerated; his judgments of my work have been distorted. He disliked *Nineteen*

Five and *Lieutenant Schmidt* and thought that I ought never to have written them; he liked two of my books, *Above the Barriers* and *My Sister, Life*.

I won't go into the history of our agreements and disagreements. I will only try, so far as possible, to give a general impression of Mayakovsky and of his significance. Naturally, it will be partial and subjectively coloured.

* * *

To start with the most important: We have no conception of the inner torture which precedes suicide. People who are physically tortured on the rack keep losing consciousness, their suffering is so great that its unendurable intensity shortens the end. But a man who is thus at the mercy of the executioner is not annihilated when he faints from pain, for he is present at his own end, his past belongs to him, his memories are his and, if he chooses, he can make use of them, they can help him before his death.

But a man who decides to commit suicide puts a full stop to his being, he turns his back on his past, he declares himself a bankrupt and his memories to be unreal. They can no longer help or save him, he has put himself beyond their reach. The continuity of his inner life is broken, his personality is at an end. And perhaps what finally makes him kill himself is not the firmness of his resolve but the unbearable quality of this anguish which belongs to no one, of this suffering in the absence of the sufferer, of this waiting which is empty because life has stopped and can no longer fill it.

It seems to me that Mayakovsky shot himself out of pride, because he condemned something in himself, or close to him, to which his self-respect could not submit. That Yesenin hanged himself without having properly thought out the consequences of his act, still saying in his inmost heart: "Who knows? Perhaps this isn't yet the end. Nothing is yet decided." That Marina Tsvetayeva had always held her work between herself and the reality of daily life; and when she found this luxury beyond her means, when she felt that for her son's sake she must, for a time, give up her passionate absorption in poetry and look round her soberly, she saw chaos, no longer screened by art, fixed, unfamiliar, motionless, and, not knowing where to run for terror, she hid in death, putting her neck into the noose as she might have hidden her head under her pillow. It seems to me that Paolo Yashvili was utterly confused, spellbound by the Shigalyovshchina [23] of 1937 as by witchcraft; and that he watched his daughter as she slept at night and, imagining himself unworthy to look at her, went out in the morning to his friends' house and blasted his head with grapeshot from his double-barrelled gun. And it seems to me that Fadeyev, still with the apologetic smile which had somehow stayed with him through all the crafty ins and outs of politics, told himself just before he pulled the trigger: "Well, now it's all over. Good-bye, Sasha."[24]

What is certain is that they all suffered beyond description, to the point where suffering has become a mental sickness. And, as we bow in homage to their gifts and to their bright memory, we should bow compassionately before their suffering.

* * *

But to come back to the summer of 1914 and to the coffee-house in the Arbat[25] where it was intended that our two literary factions should clash. Bobrov and I had been sent to represent our side; Tretyakov and Shershenevich, who represented theirs, brought Mayakovsky with them.

It turned out that I knew him by sight. We had been to the same school, though he had been my junior by two years,[26] and I had also seen him at concerts.

A few days earlier a man who was later to become one of his blind followers showed me some newly published verses of Mayakovsky's. So little did this future disciple understand his god at the time that he laughed at them and was indignant as at an obvious piece of giftless nonsense. But the poem had attracted me immensely. It was one of his most brilliant early experiments, and was afterwards included in *As Simple as Mooing*.[27]

Now, at the café, I found that I liked the author no less than I had liked his verse. Before me sat a handsome, sombre youth with a boxer's fists, the deep voice of an Archdeacon and an inexhaustible, deadly wit—something between one of Alexander Grin's mythical heroes and a Spanish toreador.

He was handsome, witty, talented—perhaps even superlatively talented, but you knew at once that these were not the most important things about him; the important thing was his iron mastery over himself, the rules or principles of honour, the sense of duty which prevented him from being any different, any less handsome, talented or witty than he was.

His resolute expression and the mane of hair which stood on end as he ruffled it with all five fingers, immediately reminded me of some young terrorist conspirator out of a Dostoyevsky novel, some minor Dostoyevsky character from the provinces.

It was not always to their disadvantage that the provinces lagged behind the capitals. In periods when the great cities fell into decline, the far-out regions were sometimes rescued by the survival in them of their virtuous past. Thus, into the kingdom of the tango and of skating rinks, Mayakovsky had brought from the remote forests of Transcaucasia where he was born the conviction, still unshaken in that forgotten corner of the world, that enlightenment in Russia could only be revolutionary.

To his natural advantages he added an artistic disorder, draping himself in a certain rough and careless clumsiness of mind and body and assuming the role of a bohemian rebel, which he acted with supreme taste. His taste was so experienced and mature that it seemed older than himself. He was twenty-two while his taste was at least a hundred and twenty-two.

* * *

I was very fond of Mayakovsky's early lyrics. Against the contemporary background of affectation and fooling, their gravity—heavy, menacing, complaining—stood out remarkably. It was poetry moulded by a master; proud and dæmonic and at the same time infinitely doomed, at the point of death, almost an appeal for help.

Time I beg: though you are blind and the
holy images you paint are daubs,
Daub my likeness into the tabernacle of our
misshapen time.
I am as lonely as the only eye
Of the one-eyed man walking towards the blind.

Time obediently did as he asked. His image is included in the tabernacle of our time. But what a gift of prophecy was needed to foreknow it then! Or take another passage:

Is it for you to understand why,
Serenely, through storms of mockery,
I bear my soul upon a dish
To feed the future . . .

" Let all flesh be still and all men stand in fear and trembling and let no earthly thought be conceived. The King of kings and the Lord of lords comes to lay down his life and to give himself to be the food of the faithful."[28] It is impossible to miss the liturgical parallel.

Unlike the "classical" writers who attached importance to the meaning of prayers and psalms, unlike Pushkin who retold St. Ephraim in his " Desert Fathers" and Alexey Tolstoy who paraphrased the requiem prayers of St. John Damascene in verse,[29]

Rainer Maria Rilke

Marina Tsvetayeva

Blok, Mayakovsky and Yesenin quoted textual passages from the prayers and psalms chanted in church and used them side by side with random words of current speech and other fragments of everyday reality picked up at home or in the street.

These quarries of ancient art prompted Mayakovsky to give a parodic structure to his poems. His poetry abounds in analogies with theological concepts, at times implicit, at others stressed. The use of this material called for hugeness, it needed a strong pair of hands and it trained the poet's daring.

It is good that neither Mayakovsky nor Yesenin turned away from what they still remembered having known in childhood—good that they dug this familiar ground, extracted its beauty and made use of it instead of leaving it buried.

* * *

When I came to know Mayakovsky better I discovered certain unexpected points of similarity in our technique—in the structure of our images for example, and in our use of rhyme. His poetry delighted me by the beauty and felicity of its movement. I could have asked for nothing better for myself. I wished neither to repeat what he was doing nor to seem to copy him; I repressed instead those tendencies in myself which echoed his—the striving for effects and the heroic tone, which in my case would have been false. This helped me to restrain and purify my style.

As a poet, Mayakovsky was not isolated, he was not a voice crying in a desert; he had neighbours and competitors. Before the revolution Igor Severyanin was his rival on the stage. In the arena of the people's revolution and in people's hearts his rival was Sergey Yesenin.

Severyanin was the king of the concert halls and, in stage terms, "always sure to fill the house". He warbled his poems to the accompaniment of two or three tunes taken from French operas and managed to be neither vulgar nor offensive to the ear.

His backwardness, his slick verbal innovations and his lack of taste, combined with his enviably pure and fluent poetic diction, created a new and curious genre —a banal version of the delayed impact of the Turgenev cult on poetry.

As for Sergey Yesenin, never since Koltsov had Russia given birth to anything more natural, intrinsic, fitting and generic to her than his talent. Light, free, unburdened by the weight of conscious application which clogged the populists, he was Russia's magnificently lavish gift to us. And with all this, Yesenin was a living part of that high tradition which, after Pushkin, we should call Mozartian

—the Mozartian principle in art, the Mozartian climate.

Yesenin treated his life like a fairytale. Like Prince Ivan, he leapt across the seas mounted on his grey wolf and captured his fire-bird,[30] Isadora Duncan.

So too, he used magic recipes for making poetry, now playing patience with his words, now writing them with his life's blood. Best of all in him was his vision of his native countryside, the Central-Russian forest country near Ryazan, a vision which he conveyed with overwhelming freshness, as it had come to him in childhood.

Mayakovsky's talent was heavier and rougher than Yesenin's, but perhaps it had more depth and a wider grasp. He was the poet, not of nature like Yesenin, but of the labyrinth of the great modern city in which the lonely spirit of our time, whose passionate, dramatic and inhuman situations he describes, has become confused and lost its way.

*   *   *

As I have said, I had less in common with Mayakovsky than was often thought. One day, when we were arguing at Aseyev's and our disagreement grew particularly sharp, Mayakovsky defined the difference between us with his usual humour: " It's true that we are different," he told me, "you prefer lightning to be in the sky, and I prefer it in an electric iron."

I could see no point in his propagandist zeal, in his determination to force himself and his companions on the attention of the public, in his campaigning, his industrial team spirit in poetry, or his submission to the voice of actuality.

Still less could I see the point of his paper, *Lef*,[31] of the composition of its board or of its system of ideas. The only honest and consistent member of this group of dissenters was Tretyakov who at least drew logical conclusions from his premises. Like Plato he believed that there could be no room for art in a young socialist state, at any rate at its inception. Certainly the pseudo-art which flourished in the pages of *Lef*—mechanical, uncreative, ruined by editorial corrections made to fit the times—was never worth the care and effort spent on it and could easily have been spared.

From his *Mystery Buffo* onwards and apart from his last and deathless document, *Full Voice*, I could make nothing of Mayakovsky's later poetry. I could make nothing of its clumsy, rhyming dictums, its elaborate triteness, its hackneyed commonplaces or their dull, confused, affected exposition. None of this, to my mind, had anything to do with Mayakovsky—there was no Mayakovsky in it. And yet astonishingly, it is this non-existent Mayakovsky who came to be regarded as revolutionary.

All the same, people continued to think of us, mistakenly, as friends. When, for instance, Yesenin was dissatisfied with imagism and wished to make his peace with Mayakovsky, he chose me as an intermediary (thinking me best fitted for this role) and asked me to arrange a meeting with him.

Although I addressed Mayakovsky as "you" and Yesenin as "thou", I saw even less of Yesenin than of Mayakovsky. I could count my meetings with Yesenin on my fingers, and they always ended in a fantastic scene. Either we swore friendship and shed floods of tears or we fought and people had to drag us apart.

* * *

In the last years of Mayakovsky's life, when there was no more poetry, neither his nor anyone's, after Yesenin had hanged himself, when, to put it plainly, writing was at an end (for the beginning of *Quiet Flows the Don* had still been poetry, and so had been the early writings of Pilnyak, Babel, Fedin and Vsevolod Ivanov)[32]—in those years, Aseyev, a good comrade and a gifted and intelligent man who retained his inward freedom and refused to blind himself to anything, was Mayakovsky's mainstay and his closest friend, nearest to him in mind.

Our ways had parted for good.[33] The reason for our final break was that although I had resigned both as a contributor to *Lef* and as a member of its group, my name continued to be printed on the list of its supporters; I wrote sharply to Mayakovsky and my letter must have made him furious.

Much earlier, while I was still under the spell of his inward strength, enthusiasm and immense claims and possibilities as an artist, and while he returned my liking with equal warmth, I had sent him my book, *My Sister, Life*, with the following lines included in the dedication:

> You are concerned about our balance sheet,
> The tragedy of the S.C.P.E.,[34]
> You who like a Flying Dutchman
> Sang in all the skies of poetry!
> I know, you are sincere,
> But what, along the path
> Of your sincerity, has brought you
> Beneath the vaults of this old people's home?

* * *

Two famous dictums were made concerning this period.[35] One was that life was better, life was merrier than in the past; the other that Mayakovsky had been and remained the best and the most gifted poet of our era. I wrote personally to thank the author for the second of these statements, for it protected me from the inflation of my role; this began about the time of the Writers' Congress in the middle 'thirties.[36] I am satisfied with my life and fond of it. I like it as it is, without any extra gold leaf. Nothing is further from my mind than a life stripped of privacy and anonymity and displayed in the glass glitter of a showcase.

Mayakovsky began to be introduced forcibly, like potatoes under Catherine the Great. This was his second death. He had no hand in it.

CHAPTER FIVE

Three Shadows

IT was in July 1917 that Ehrenburg sought me out on the advice of Bryusov. That was how I came to know this clever writer, a man whose make-up, active and sociable, is the opposite of mine.

This was the beginning of the big influx of Russians who were coming home—former emigrants from the Old Régime, people whom the outbreak of the war had found abroad and who had been interned, and others. Andrey Bely, who had come from Switzerland, and Ehrenburg were among them.

Ehrenburg spoke very highly of Tsvetayeva and showed me her poems.[1] Once at the beginning of the revolution I heard her read her verses at a meeting; she was one of several speakers on the platform. Another time, in winter, during the period of War Communism,[2] I went to see her on some errand; I spoke of trifles and she spoke of trifles in reply. I could make nothing of her work.

At that time, my ear was vitiated by our verbal whirligigs and the twisting and chopping of all familiar things which was going on everywhere. Anything said in a normal way bounced off me. I forgot that words could have a sense and content of their own, without the tinkling ornaments we hung on them.

The very harmony of Tsvetayeva's poems, their clear meaning, the fact that they had only merits and there was nothing wrong with them, were to me an obstacle and prevented me from seeing their point. I wasn't looking for the point of things, only for their incidental sharpness.

I continued to underrate Tsvetayeva for a long time, just as in different ways I underrated many others—Bagritsky, Khlebnikov, Mandelstamm, Gumilyov.

I have already said that while the rest of us were still so tongue-tied that we could only be original despite ourselves and make a virtue of our inarticulateness, Aseyev and Tsvetayeva spoke like human beings and used a classical style and language in writing.

There came a day when both of them gave up their skill: Aseyev was seduced by Khlebnikov's example and Tsvetayeva went through an inner transformation of her own. But by then I had fallen under the charm of the earlier, traditional, unregenerate Tsvetayeva.

*   *   *

You had to read your way into her. When I had done this, I was amazed by her boundless strength and purity. There was nothing like it anywhere else. To put it briefly—I can honestly say that if you except Annensky, Blok and with certain reservations Bely, Tsvetayeva's early manner was exactly what all the symbolists, from first to last, dreamed of and did not achieve. And while they spluttered helplessly in their linguistic ocean of lifeless schemes and dead archaic forms, Tsvetayeva soared over the real difficulties of creation, solving its problems effortlessly and with matchless technical skill.

It was not until the spring of 1922, after she had left Russia, that I came across a volume of her *Versty* in a Moscow bookshop. I was immediately overcome by the immense lyrical power of her poetic form. It was a form which had sprung living from experience—personal, and neither narrow-chested nor short of breath from line to line but rich and compact and enveloping whole sequences of stanza after stanza in its vast periods of unbroken rhythm.

I felt a kinship with something which lay beyond

these individual qualities—an experience, perhaps, of the same influences, or of common factors in the formation of character, such as the role of home and music in my life, a similarity of points of departure, tastes and aspirations.

Tsvetayeva was in Prague. I sent her an enthusiastic letter, full of my astonishment at failing to appreciate her for so long and at discovering her so late. She replied, and we went on exchanging letters. Our correspondence became more frequent in the middle 'twenties, when her *Craft* was published, and when her *End Poem, Hill Poem* and *Ratcatcher*—all vast in scope and meaning, vivid and magnificently new—were seen in manuscript in Moscow. That was how we became friends.

In the summer of 1935,[3] when I was on the verge of mental illness after almost twelve months of insomnia, I found myself at an anti-Fascist congress in Paris. There I met Tsvetayeva's son and daughter and her husband, an enchanting, sensitive and steadfast being of whom I grew as fond as of a brother.

Tsvetayeva's family were pressing her to return to Russia. It was partly that they were homesick, partly that they sympathised with Communism and the Soviet Union; and partly that they thought Tsvetayeva had no sort of life in Paris and was going to pieces in loneliness and isolation from her readers.

She asked me what I thought about it. I had no definite opinion. It was hard to know what to advise them; I was afraid that these remarkable people would have a difficult and troubled time at home. But the tragedy which was to strike the whole family surpassed my fears beyond all measure.

* * *

When I was speaking of my childhood at the beginning of this sketch, I described actual events and scenes, but further on I confined myself to generalities and brief impressions. I had to do this for lack of space.

If I were to tell the story of my friendship with Tsvetayeva incident by incident and step by step, including all the interests and hopes which brought us together, I would soon outrun the limits I have set myself. It would need a whole book, so much did we experience together—so many changes, joys and tragedies, always unexpected and always widening our horizons.

But here, as in what remains to be said, I will keep away from personal and private things and mention only what is general and essential.

Tsvetayeva had an active, virile, militant soul, resolute and indomitable. Both in life and art she had an eager, avid, almost a rapacious need for definition and finality, and in pursuing this she outstripped everyone else.

Apart from her few known works she wrote many others which are unknown in Russia, huge, stormy compositions, some in the style of Russian folk-lore, others on general historic, mythological and legendary themes.

Their publication will be a triumph and a revelation for our native poetry which, in a single moment, will be enriched by all these overdue gifts.

I believe that the re-evaluation and the recognition which await Tsvetayeva will be very great.

We were friends. I had almost a hundred of her letters, written in reply to mine. For all that I have said of the importance in my life of things vanished or lost, I could never have imagined that I would lose these priceless and treasured letters. I lost them through excessive care to keep them safe.

During the war, when I used to visit my family in the country to which they had been evacuated, a member of the staff of the Scriabin Museum, who was a great friend of mine and a great admirer of Tsvetayeva, offered to look after them together with some letters from my parents and a few from Gorky and Romain Rolland. She put them in the safe of the Museum—all except Tsvetayeva's; these she kept by her, never letting them out of her sight and not even trusting them to the fireproof safe.

She lived all the year round in the country and took the letters with her every day, in a small attaché-case, to and from her work. One winter's evening she was going home utterly exhausted. When she was half-way home from the country station, walking through the wood, she realised that she had left the case in the coach of the suburban train. That was how Tsvetayeva's letters were borne away and vanished.

* * *

Over the decades since the publication of *Safe Conduct*, I have often thought that, should it ever be reprinted, I would add a chapter about the Caucasus and about two Georgian poets. Time passed and this gap remained unfilled. Now I will write this account.

It was in winter, in about 1930, that the poet Paolo Yashvili and his wife came to see me in Moscow. He was brilliant, polished, cultured, an amusing talker, European and good-looking.

Soon after this, there were painful upheavals, changes and complications which involved two families, my own and that of some friends of mine. For a long time neither I nor my companion, who was later to become my second wife,[4] had anywhere to lay our heads. Yashvili offered us a refuge in his house in Tiflis.[5]

In those days I knew nothing about the Caucasus or Georgia, nothing about the Georgians or their life. It was all a complete revelation to me. Everything was unfamiliar and everything was astonishing. The huge dark stormy mountains looming at the end of every street in Tiflis. The home life of the poor carried on out of doors, bolder, less in hiding, more frank and vivid than in the north. The popular traditions filled with mystical and messianic symbols, disposing everyone to live in his imagination and, as in Catholic Poland,[6] making of everyone a poet. The high level of culture of the leading section of society—an active intellectual life which, by then, was rarely to be found elsewhere. The better districts of the town recalling Petersburg, their ground-floor window bars bent into the shapes of lyres and flower-baskets; the picturesque back streets. The beat of tambourines, drumming the Lezginka, perpetually at your heels and overtaking you at every turn. The goat-like bleating of bagpipes, and the sound of other instruments. The advent of the evening in a southern town, full of stars, and of the smells of gardens, pastry-shops and coffee-houses.

Yashvili was a remarkable poet of the post-symbolist period. His verse is built on the precise and carefully established evidence of the senses. It has affinities with the modern European prose of Bely, Hamsun, Proust, and, like their prose, it has the freshness of sharp and unexpected observations. It is supremely creative, not cluttered up with tightly packed effects, but airy, spacious, full of breath and movement.

* * *

The outbreak of the First World War found Yashvili in Paris where he was studying at the Sorbonne. He set out for home by a roundabout way. At a small station in Norway he missed his train. A young Norwegian and his wife, who had come by sleigh from some remote farm to fetch the mail, noticed the predicament of the fiery southerner and took pity on him. They managed somehow to communicate with him and carried him off to their farm to wait for the next train which was not due until the following day.

Yashvili told stories wonderfully. He was a born teller of adventure tales. He was always getting into unexpected situations, and they always had the style of a well written short story. Chance happenings positively sought him out and clung to him; he had a lucky hand with them, it was his special gift.

Talent radiated from him. His eyes shone with an inner fire; the fire of passion had scorched his lips and the heat of experience had burnt and blackened his face, so that he looked older than his years and as though he had been worn and tattered by life.

On the day we arrived he gathered his friends, members of a group of which he was the leader. I don't remember who was there that time. Probably his next-door neighbour, Nikolay Nadiradze, a genuine and first-rate lyric poet. And Titsian Tabidze and his wife.

* * *

I remember that room as if it were to-day. How indeed could I forget it? Carefully, not to shatter its image—before I knew what terrors were reserved for it—I let it sink that very evening to the bottom of my soul, with all the frightful things that later were to happen in it and around it.

Why were these two people sent to me? How is our relationship to be described? They have become an integral part of my personal life. I could not choose between them, I did not prefer either of them to the other, so inseparable were they and so perfectly did they complement each other.

The fate of these two men and of Tsvetayeva was to be my greatest sorrow.

* * *

If the expression of Yashvili's personality was outward-looking, extrovert, Tabidze was withdrawn into himself, and his every line and his every gesture were an invitation into the interior of his soul, rich in intuition and presentiment.

The astonishing thing about his poetry was the feeling it conveyed of unexhausted lyrical reserves, the feeling that the unspoken and what remained for him to say outweighed everything he had already said. This sense of still untouched resources of the spirit was the background of his verse, it gave it added depth and that specific mood which held it and which is its great and bitter charm. There is as much soul in his poetry as there was in him, a reserved and complicated soul, wholly attracted to the good and capable of clairvoyance and self-sacrifice.

Thinking of Yashvili I think of urban situations—rooms, arguments, public meetings, Yashvili sparkling with eloquence at crowded parties at night.

The memory of Tabidze puts me in mind of the country; landscapes rise in my imagination, the waves of the sea and a vast flowering plain.

I remember clouds drifting in a row and, behind them in the distance, mountains rising to the same level. Merging into this background is the stocky, thick-set figure of the smiling poet. He has a jerky step and when he laughs his whole body shakes. Now he rises, turns sideways to the table and knocks his knife against a tumbler calling for silence—he is about to make a speech. His habit of raising one shoulder higher than the other gives him a lop-sided look.

The house in Kodzhory [7] stood on a slope, and the road, looping its way uphill, passed it, turned and went on climbing past its windows at the back; so that those who walked or drove along the road could be seen from the house twice.

This was at the time when, according to Bely, the triumph of materialism had done away with all material things. There was nothing to eat or to put on. There was nothing tangible, nothing existed except ideas. If we kept alive, it was thanks to our Caucasian friends who performed miracles for our benefit, getting and bringing us what we needed most, and raising loans for us from publishers against our non-existent assets. . . .

We are all gathered together, we share our news, have supper and read aloud to one another. A small, fresh wind quickly runs its fingers over the silver poplar leaves, turning them over and showing their white velvet linings. The air is as full of sleepy southern fragrance as of rumours. And high up, like any cart turning on its axle, the night slowly turns its lumbering wagon of stars. And people, cars and carts move along the road, and everyone is seen from the house twice.

Or we are on the Georgian Military Highway, or at Borzhóm or at Abastumán. Or, after journeys, sights, adventures, drinks, we are at Bakuryány (I, for my part, with a black eye from having fallen flat on my face) at the house of Leonidze, the most independent of all poets, the one closest to the secrets of his language and therefore least translatable.

We picnic in the woods at night; Leonidze has a beautiful wife and two small, enchanting daughters. And next day a *mestvir*—a wandering minstrel—comes with his bagpipes and improvises a poem in honour of each guest as we all sit round the table, seizing on every pretext for a toast—even my black eye will serve.

Or we are staying by the sea at Kobulety; it rains and storms, and in the same hotel with us is young

Simon Chikovani, the future master of a brilliant visual poetic style. We walk together, and always beside me, and above the line of mountains and horizons, I see the smiling poet's head, and the bright signs of his outstanding gifts and the shadow of sadness and destiny about him. And as I take my leave of him once again, let me, in his person, take leave of all my other memories.

CHAPTER SIX

Conclusion

HERE I end my sketch. I am not cutting it short or leaving it unfinished. I am ending it exactly where I meant to end it from the very first. I had no intention of writing the history of half a century in many volumes and with many characters.

There are many good poets whom I have not included in my sketch—Martynov, Zabolotsky, Selvinsky, Tikhonov—all good poets. I have not said anything about the poets of the generation of Simonov and Tvardovsky, which counts so many of them.

I have deliberately kept within the narrowest circle of my life, limiting myself to this.

What I have written is enough to give some idea of how, in my individual case, life became converted into art and art was born of life and of experience.

I have already said how divided is my attitude to my poetic past—my own and that of many others. I would not lift a finger to rescue more than a quarter of my writings from oblivion. Why then have I agreed to have a collection of my poems published?[1]

There are two reasons. One is that, for all that spoils them and that saddens and annoys me in them, they do contain some particles of what they should contain—a few exact and successful discoveries.

The other is that I have just finished my chief and most important work, the only one of which I am not ashamed and for which I take full responsibility, a novel in prose with a section in verse, *Doctor Zhivago*.

The poems scattered over the past years of my life and collected in the present book are steps preparatory to the novel. And it is as a preparation for the novel that I regard their publication in this book.

* * *

Here ends my biographical sketch. To take it further would be immeasurably difficult. If I went on with it, keeping to the sequence of events, I would have to speak of years and circumstances, of people and of destinies contained within the framework of the revolution. Of a world of aims and aspirations, problems and achievements previously unknown, and of a new restraint, a new severity and new trials which it imposed on human personality, pride, honour, industry and endurance.

This world, unique and not to be compared with

any other, has now withdrawn into the distance of memory; it looms on the horizon like mountains seen from a plain, or like a distant city smoking in its night glow.

To write of it one should write in such a way as to make the hair rise and the heart falter. To write of it by rote and habit, to write less than overwhelmingly, to write less vividly than Gogol or Dostoyevsky wrote of Petersburg, would be not only without sense or purpose—it would be base and shameless.

We are still far from this ideal way of writing.

NOTES

Compiled by V. F.

CHAPTER ONE

1. i.e. 10th February, 1890. In the nineteenth century the "Old" (i.e. Julian Calendar) lagged 12 days behind the Gregorian Calendar which was not introduced in Russia until 1918. In the twentieth century the difference was 13 days. In these notes, both dates are given until 1918.
2. Wet-nurses stayed with children longer than in the West and were a usual and showy sight when they took their charges for walks, as they wore the national dress including the *Kokoshnik* (diadem embroidered with artificial pearls) and many rows of coloured beads.
3. Tverskiye-Yamskiye: literally, Tver coach service streets. The Pipe: Truba Square. Tsvetnoy: Flower Boulevard. There was a flea-market in the Truba. The neighbourhood was one of slums and vice, with whole streets of brothels. (cf. *Doctor Zhivago*, pp. 411–12.) See Map on p. 31.
4. Literally: "School of Painting, Sculpture and Architecture." The school was founded in 1832 as an "Art Group", became a college in 1843, and was amalgamated with the Imperial College of Architecture in 1863.
5. Mentioned in guide-books of the period as a lively street with well-to-do private houses and foreign shops. Now called Kirov Street. See Map on p. 31.
6. The fire which broke out immediately after the occupation of Moscow by Napoleon.
7. L. N. Tolstoy.
8. In fact Chaikovsky died in November 1893 and Anton Rubinstein in November 1894.
9. On 9th November, 1863, thirteen pupils of the Academy of Art, all Gold Medallist candidates, refused to paint a picture on the set subject of "Odin in Valhalla". They

formed an Artists' Co-operative Society, and, assisted financially by a rich patron of the arts, Tretyakov, founded in 1870 the Society for Travelling Art Exhibitions. (*Peredvizhniki*). The society, which received ideological support from the writings of V. V. Stasov, undertook to educate the masses by means of exhibitions, held in the capitals and the main cities such as Riga, Kazan, etc. Members of the society included the brothers Vasnetsov, Levitan, V. E. Makovsky, Polenov, Repin, Serov, Surikov. The society deeply influenced contemporary Russian taste; indeed its concept of art as a means of persuasion, its insistence on "realism" and the priority it accorded to content at the expense of form, still determine the views of most educated Russians to-day.

10. Repin, Myasoyedov, Makovsky, Surikov, Polenov. cf. Index of names. (For the convenience of the English reader, lists of Russian names which may be unknown to him have occasionally been omitted from the text and included in these notes.)
11. Serov, Levitan, Korovin, Vrubel, Ivanov. (cf. preceding note.)
12. The Union was formed in 1903 by a group of painters who, on the average, were twenty years younger than their social-minded predecessors and were more tolerant of modern European influences. A number of them had seceded from the Peredvizhniki.
13. Illustrated weekly published in Petersburg from 1870 to 1918. Its publisher (Adolf Fyodorovich Marx, 1839–1904) made the circulation soar to over 200,000 by printing free supplements of complete editions of Russian and foreign classics. Tolstoy's *Resurrection* was serialised in 1899, Nos. 11 to 52.
14. For prisoners being deported to Siberia.

CHAPTER TWO

1. Known as the " forty forties ": a poetic exaggeration as Moscow never had 1600 churches, though in the mid-nineteenth century it had 370, for 380,000 inhabitants.
2. According to a theory which became current after the Grand Dukes of Russia had assumed the title of Tsars, Moscow (the capital of Russia from the fourteenth to the eighteenth century) was the Third Rome. (The "First Rome" was the Roman Empire, the " Second " was Byzantium.)
3. Saints of the Orthodox Church martyred in Illyria in the second century because they erected a cross on a heathen temple which they had been ordered to build. Their feast day is the 15th August. See Map on p. 31.
4. Saints Peter and Paul Gymnasium, attached to the Moscow Lutheran Church, founded for children of the resident German community, but was also used by many Russian and Russian-Jewish Moscow families.
5. Pyotr Semyonovich Vannovsky (1822–1904), Minister of Education (1901 and 1902), modernised secondary education, putting less stress on ancient languages and more on science.
6. Small furnished country house. The school holidays in Russia last from mid-May to mid-August and many middle-class families took *dachas* for the whole of this period. Both Leonid Pasternak and Scriabin were teachers and had equally long holidays.
7. Russian equivalent of " Mr. Smith ".
8. A character in Griboyedov's comedy, *The Misfortune of being Clever*, which ends with the snob Famusov sighing: " But what will Princess Maria Alexevna say? "
9. 1904–09.
10. *V nochnoye*. It was usual in summer for village children to take horses to night pastures, often far from the village.

Turgenev describes such a scene in his story *The Bezhin Meadow*.

11. i.e. roughly 1897–1907.
12. Literally: "harmonic Promethean summer lightnings". Scriabin's *Prometheus, Symphonic Poem on the theme of Fire* (1909–10) was to be accompanied by intricate light effects. Scriabin himself devised and built a complicated projector for this purpose.

CHAPTER THREE

1. Because of the strikes and revolutionary disorders which occurred during the Russo-Japanese War of 1904–05, Nicholas II was persuaded by his advisers to issue The Manifesto of 17th October, which promised a constitutional régime. But on the day it was issued a procession of students carrying red flags was attacked by Cossacks; one student was killed. His funeral procession a few days later turned into a mass demonstration by students and workers and that evening Cossacks and "Black Hundreds" (members of the "Union of the Russian People") beat up and killed a number of students. (The "Union" was an organisation formed by reactionary anti-Semitic groups; it agitated for the restoration of autocracy and, with the connivance of the police, organised anti-Jewish pogroms and attacks on students who were a traditionally revolutionary body.)
2. The game market district of central Moscow where the Union recruited its rank and file.
3. The final stage of the conflict, which culminated in the general strike, lasted in Moscow from 9th (22nd) to 19th December, 1905 (1st January, 1906).
4. *The Scourge: Bich: the Bugaboo: Zhupel.*
5. An exhibition of Leonid Pasternak's paintings was held in Berlin in spring 1906.

6. "Pussywillows" (*Verbochki*) was first published in the journal *Tropinka*, No. 6, 1906. *Childhood* (*Detstvo*) appeared in the almanac *Grif*, 1904.
7. These quatrains are taken from poems dated respectively 6th (19th) August, 1902, 26th October (8th November), 1907, and 4th (17th) October, 1910.
8. The cycle *The Terrible World* (*Strashny Mir*) belongs to the period 1909–16; the rest of the poems mentioned were written in 1904–05. They reflect Blok's obsession with the big city (Petersburg) and its inhumanity, particularly towards women.
9. Bryusov, Andrey Bely, Khodasevich, Vyacheslav, Ivanov, Baltrushaytis. (cf. Note 10, p. 124.)
10. i.e. between 1st and 9th May, 1921.
11. Blok died on 7th August, 1921.
12. *Die Geheimnisse* (1785), an unfinished epic poem.
13. Winter of 1903–04.
14. The New Drama Theatre founded by the famous actress and producer, Komissarzhevskaya.
15. Gorky, obliged to emigrate as a result of his revolutionary activities in 1905, had stopped in Berlin on his way to the U.S.A.
16. Pasternak described his first meeting with Rilke in *Safe Conduct* which he dedicated to Rilke's memory. Rilke was in Russia from 27th April to 18th June, 1899 (when he first met L. Pasternak) and from 1st May to 22nd August, 1900. Two letters to Leonid Pasternak are published in Rilke's *Briefe aus den Jahren* 1892 *bis* 1904, Leipzig, 1939. Another letter (14th March, 1926), written after L. Pasternak had emigrated to Germany, is included in Rilke's *Gesammelte Briefe in Sechs Bänden*, Vol. V, Leipzig, 1937.
17. There follow Pasternak's translations of Rilke's poems "Der Lesende" and "Der Schauende" (*Gesammelte Werke*, Vol. III, 1927, pp. 135 and 137–8).
18. The Golden Fleece (*Zolotoye Runo*) was a symbolist monthly, patronised by the millionaire N. I. Ryabushinsky, which

appeared in Moscow from 1906 to 1909 and sponsored exhibitions of modern painting. The Knave of Diamonds (*Buvnovy Valet*) was a painters' association which existed from 1910 to 1926. The Donkey's Tail (*Osliny Khvost*) was the name of a group of futurist painters. The Blue Rose (*Golubaya Rosa*) was an impressionist exhibition held in Moscow in 1907.

19. *Samorodok:* literally "nugget". (Although the nearest English equivalent is "rough diamond", *samorodok* has not the implication of "roughness").
20. *Musaget* (i.e. Musagetes, Apollo, leader of the Muses) a publishing house, founded in 1909; published a symbolist review of the same name.
21. Andrey Bely, Stepun, Rachinsky, Boris Sadovsky, Emile Medtner, Shenrok, Petrovsky, Ellis, Nilender. (cf. Note 10, p. 124.)
22. Tolstoy left Yasnaya Polyana in the early morning of 28th October (10th November), 1910, travelling third class by train, and died of pneumonia at the stationmaster's house at Astapovo on 7th (20th) November, 1910.
23. Tolstoy's widow.
24. The antagonism between Tolstoy's disciples, who surrounded him, and his wife, poisoned his last years and contributed to his decision to leave home.
25. *Pushkin's Duel and his Death* (*Duel i Smert Pushkina*) by P. Y. Shchegolev, 1936 (amended edition). Pushkin married Natalya Nikolayevna, née Goncharova, on 18th February, 1831, when she was only sixteen. There were two sons and two daughters of this marriage. Pushkin was killed on 29th January, 1837, in a duel with a cavalry officer, Dantès, an adopted son of the Dutch ambassador, whom he suspected of being his wife's lover. The background to this episode has been a ceaseless subject of discussion among Russian writers and literary historians.
26. The argument in the last two paragraphs seems to be that the Tolstoyans misunderstood Tolstoy through treating his

view as an abstraction, just as scholars of Pushkin have missed the point of Pushkin by making an abstraction of his case.

CHAPTER FOUR

1. cf. *Safe Conduct* where that summer is described in greater detail.
2. Literally: an aristocratic way of mispronouncing *r*.
3. The revival of Kant's philosophy by Herman Cohen and other Marburg philosophers greatly influenced Russian idealist philosophers at the time.
4. Dmitry Samarin's grandfather, Yury Fyodorovich Samarin (1819–76), was a leader of the Slavophil movement (opposed to the "Westernisers" who favoured Western influence on Russian culture).
5. Where Pasternak has been living since the 'thirties. In his poem "The Old Park", in the collection *On Early Trains* (*Na Rannikh Poyezdakh*), 1941, Pasternak describes a wounded Soviet officer who is brought to a hospital which he recognises as the old country house of his family, the Samarins. The poem seems to refer to a son of Pasternak's friend Dmitry.
6. New Economic Policy (of relaxation) introduced by Lenin in 1921.
7. 1913.
8. Literally: "romantic affection and making myself interesting in extraneous ways" (i.e. ways irrelevant to the content of the poems).
9. Literally: "the West would be disclosed in the manœuvres of storms [or misfortunes] and railway sleepers."
10. A historical monthly published in Moscow, 1863–1917.
11. Some of these early poems, including "Venice" and "The Railway Station", were later thoroughly revised by Pas-

ternak and included in the collected poems published in the 'twenties and 'thirties.

12. A tributary of the Volga.
13. *Kamerny Teatr,* founded by A. Tairov in Moscow in 1914 in reaction against the realism of the Stanislavsky Theatre.
14. A leading Moscow manufacturer of haberdashery.
15. Einem was a chocolate manufacturer; Ferrein was the largest pharmacological establishment in Russia.
16. In fact, *Plantain* (*Podorozhnik*) did not appear until 1921. Pasternak must have been reading either *Vecher* (*Evening*), 1912, or *Chotki* (*Rosary*), 1913.
17. The two winters are presumably those of 1915–16 and 1916–17. Pasternak's poems *Uralskiye Stikhi* (*Urals Verses*) first published in 1922, and the chapter in *Doctor Zhivago* describing the country around "Yuryatin" reflect Pasternak's experiences in 1915–17.
18. Literally: 250 versts, i.e. about 170 miles!
19. The action of Pushkin's story *The Captain's Daughter* (1836) takes place during the Pugachov rebellion in 1773–75 in the country south of the districts where Pasternak worked, between the Urals and the Lower Volga. cf. *Doctor Zhivago* in which Zhivago writes sketches of the "Pugachev country" which he has visited.
20. An old-established ordnance factory.
21. *The Contemporary* (*Sovremennik*) appeared in Moscow 1911–15.
22. These are described more fully in *Safe Conduct*.
23. i.e. "Shigalyov methods". Shigalyov is a conspirator in Dostoyevsky's *The Possessed* who "sets out from boundless freedom and arrives at boundless despotism." According to another member of the conspiracy he says, "everyone must spy and inform on everyone else. Everyone belongs to all and all belong to everyone. All are slaves and equal in their slavery. . . . Cicero's tongue will be cut out, Copernicus will have his eyes gouged out, Shakespeare will be stoned. . . . Slaves must be equal."

24. Sasha: diminutive of Alexander (Fadeyev is addressing himself).
25. A main street in central Moscow.
26. Mayakovsky entered the Fourth Form of the Fifth Moscow High School in August 1906 and left the school by his own wish in March 1908.
27. *Prostoye kak Mychaniye,* published in 1916 by the " Parus " publishing house directed by Gorky.
28. Passage quoted from the Holy Week liturgy of the Orthodox Church.
29. The second half of Pushkin's " Desert Fathers " (1836) is a paraphrase of a penitential prayer of St. Ephraim of Syria which is recited at all the services in Lent in the Eastern Church. " Troparion ", a part of A. Tolstoy's *St. John Damascene* (1858), paraphrases the *idiomela* of St. John Damascene which forms part of the Orthodox Requiem. Both Pushkin's and Tolstoy's poems have been translated by Maurice Baring.
30. Ivan is the stock fool of Russian folk-lore. Prince Ivan with his friend and adviser, the Grey Wolf, is a character in the folk-tale " The Fire Bird ".
31. " *LEvy Front Iskustva* " (Left Front of Art), an association of futurists formed in the early days of the revolution; its journal *Lef* was published 1923–25 and revived for a short time in 1927 as *Novy Lef* (*New Lef*).
32. The first volume of the first (unexpurgated) version of M. A. Sholokhov's novel *And Quiet Flows the Don* appeared in 1928; Pilnyak's *The Naked Year* in 1922 and his *Story of the Unextinguished Moon* in 1927; Babel's *Cavalry* in 1924; Fedin's *Cities and Years* in 1924; Vsevolod Ivanov's *Armoured Train No.* 14–69 in 1922 and his *Blue Sand* in 1923.
33. There are friendly references to Pasternak in Mayakovsky's speeches as late as 1927. The final break seems to have come during the short life of *Novy Lef.*
34. Supreme Council of People's Economy (*Vysshy Soviet Narodnogo Khozyaystva*), set up in 1917 as supreme economic

organ of the dictatorship of the proletariat, and reorganised in 1932 as three bodies: The People's Commissariats of Heavy Industry, Light Industry and Timber Industry.

35. Both by Stalin.
36. First Writers' Congress, August 1934.

CHAPTER FIVE

1. Ehrenburg praises Tsvetayeva's poetry in *Literaturnaya Moskva,* 1956, pp. 709–15. An editorial note to his article announces the forthcoming publication of Tsvetayeva's verse by the State Literary Publishing House; the decision to publish it was confirmed by Surkov in May 1957 but the book has not yet appeared.
2. Years immediately following the Revolution.
3. International Congress of Anti-Fascist Writers, 21st–25th June, 1935. The Soviet delegation included Boris Pasternak, Alexey Tolstoy, I. Ehrenburg, N. S. Tikhonov, Vsevolod Ivanov and others.
4. Zinaida Neuhaus.
5. Gorky suggested in *Pravda* (31st August, 1934) that a group of Russian writers including Pasternak should go to Georgia and arrange for the translation of works by Georgian poets into Russian. Pasternak has since published a number of such translations, e.g. *Gruzinskiye Liriki* (*Georgian Lyrical Poets*) 1935, reprinted 1937, *Gruzinskiye Poety* (*Georgian Poets*), 1946, and in *Krasnaya Nov,* 1934, No. 6, pp. 3–5, and *Novy Mir,* 1956, No. 7, pp. 90–2, translations of Yashvili, Leonidze and Tabidze.
6. In a hitherto unpublished poem, "Grass and Stones", Pasternak again compares Georgia and Poland.
7. A suburb of Tiflis.

CHAPTER SIX

1. Pasternak's autobiographical essay was to be published in Russia with a collection of his poems, but the book has not so far appeared.

Alphabetical list of names mentioned in the text, with the exception of names of internationally known writers

Compiled by D. M.

AKHMATOVA, Anna, pen name of Anna Arkadyevna Gorenko, b. 1888. *Poetess.* Married Gumilyov (1910), divorced in 1918. Began to publish poetry in 1907. Love lyrics (1912–15) established her popularity. After the revolution brought out one book, *A.D. Nineteen-twenty-one* (1923), then fell silent as a poet for seventeen years, though during this period she published some important studies on Pushkin. Took advantage of the greater leniency towards writers during the Second World War to publish a selection of old and new poems in 1940. Zhdanov's attack on her in 1946 led to her expulsion from the Union of Soviet Writers. Published patriotic verse in 1950. The themes of love and death predominate in her poetry which shows some of the best qualities of acmeism.

(*Acmeism* was a movement in Russian poetry which arose in 1912. It reacted against the mysticism and vagueness of symbolist poetry and called for a return to clarity, precision and concreteness. It also emphasised the virile and heroic aspects of life.)

" ALKONOST ". Publisher of Blok's works. Vol. II of the collected works appeared in Petrograd in 1922. (*Alkonost*: magic bird with a human face in Russian folk-lore.)

ANDREYEVA, Marya Fyodorovna, 1872–1953. *Actress.* Joined Stanislavky's amateur theatrical group in 1894 and later became member of the Moscow Arts Theatre. From 1903, associated with Gorky, acting as his secretary, and travelled with him in Europe and U.S.A. Helped to organise Petrograd Bolshoy Theatre in 1919.

ANNENSKY, Innokenty Fyodorovich, 1856–1909. *Poet* and eminent classical scholar. Headmaster of famous Tsarskoe-Selo boarding-school (*lyceum*). Translated Rimbaud, Baudelaire, and the whole of Euripedes. In 1904, at the age of forty-eight, he published, under the pseudonym Nik T-o (*nikto:* "nobody") a book of lyrical poems, *Quiet Songs,* which roused great interest among the symbolist poets of the time. His second book *The Cypress Chest,* published posthumously in 1910, is usually considered to be his masterpiece. The theme of death predominates in his poetry which is constructed with great subtlety and precision. His poetic use of colloquial language foreshadows Pasternak.

ASEYEV, Nikolay Nikolayevich, b. 1889. *Poet* of the same futurist group as Mayakovsky, whom he distinguished sharply from such futurists (cf. below) as Khlebnikov. Began writing in 1913; published collections of verse during the First World War and revolutionary verses during the Civil War. Helped to found the journal *Lef* in 1923. In 1926 published notable poem on a revolutionary theme, *The Twenty-six* (i.e. the 26 Baku Commissars executed in 1918). Awarded Stalin Prize for poem in honour of Mayakovsky (1941). Wrote patriotic verses in 1941–45 and anti-American verses and songs after the war.

(Russian *Futurism* was a poetic movement initiated by Khlebnikov who, with Mayakovsky and others, published in 1912 a Manifesto entitled *A Slap in the Face of Public Taste.* The futurists, attracted by technology and other features of modern life, not only reacted against symbolism, particularly its mysticism and æstheticism, but wished to scrap the whole cultural tradition of the past and used shock tactics to bring their ideas to the attention of the public. Their journal *Lef* was intended to counteract the tendency towards a return to conservative realism.)

BABEL, Isaak Emanuilovich, 1894–1938. *Short story writer.* Born in Odessa. First stories published by Gorky in his *Annals* (1915). They were attacked as pornographic and Babel was prosecuted. Fought with Budyony's Cossack cavalry in Soviet–Polish war. Stories of early Soviet period began to appear in 1923 and won him recognition as an outstanding writer. Wrote on Polish campaign (*The Red Cavalry,* 1923) and about Odessa underworld; stories of blood and death, crime, heroism and cruelty; his irony enhances their heroic pathos. Disappeared in purge of 1937–38. In 1956 his work was re-published and discussed in Russia for the first time since 1937.

BAGRITSKY, Eduard Georgyevich, pen-name of Dzyubin, 1895–1934. *Poet.* One of the most gifted post-revolutionary poets. Wrote verses during the First World War influenced by Mayakovsky, Gumilyov and acmeism (cf. note on AHKMATOVA). Verses in the twenties deal with Civil War and life of sailors and fishermen. The setting of his major work, "The Epic of Apanas" (1926), is the Civil War in the Ukraine. Poems in the 'thirties praise the constructive work of ordinary people ("The New Knights") and especially of Soviet young people ("Death of a Pioneer Girl").

BALMONT, Konstantin Dmitryevich, 1867–1943. *Poet.* Leader of early symbolist movement. First collection of poems was published in 1894. Travelled in South Africa, Mexico, New Zealand, Spain. Translated Shelley, Whitman, E. A. Poe, Calderon. Emigrated in 1918 and died in Paris.

BALTRUSHAYTIS, Jurgis Kazimirovich, 1873–1945. *Poet.* Born in Lithuania, son of a peasant. Taught to read by village priest, then went to school, keeping himself from the age of fifteen as teacher in winter and shepherd in summer. Studied at Moscow University. Travelled in Europe and America. In 1921 became Lithuanian Chargé d'Affaires in Moscow. From 1899, wrote poetry in Russian and Lithuanian. Associated with symbolists and co-founder of their publishing house "Scorpion". Translated Byron, Ibsen, D'Annunzio, Hamsun, Wilde and Strindberg.

BELINSKY, Vissarion Grigoryevich, 1811–48. A famous *literary critic* whose ideas on the social purpose of literature greatly influenced contemporary Russian writing. First critic to appreciate Dostoyevsky. Because of his passionately polemical disposition, was nicknamed by his friends "Furious Vissarion".

BELY, Andrey, pen-name of Boris Nikolayevich Bugayev,

1880–1934. *Poet* and *novelist*. Born in Moscow, son of a professor of mathematics. Influenced by Vladimir Solovyov's mystical teaching, Bely believed that the first years of the new century were to bring a new revelation—that of the Feminine Hypostasis, Sophia—and that its coming would transfigure the world. His first writings, already showing the musical construction of his prose at its best, appeared in 1902, under the title *Symphony (Second, Dramatic);* this " Second " Symphony was followed by the *First* (1904), *Third* (1905) and *Fourth* (1908). In 1904 he began to contribute to Bryusov's journal *The Scales*. Published two novels, *The Silver Dove* (1909) and the more famous *Petersburg* (1913), which were to have an enormous influence on early Soviet prose. 1912–16: lived at Rudolf Steiner's anthroposophic centre in Switzerland, working on the construction of an anthroposophic temple and writing. On returning to Russia published *Kotik Letayev* (1917). Welcomed the Bolshevik revolution as a destructive and emancipating storm. 1918–21: engaged in many activities which included the founding of a Free Philosophical Association, courses for proletarian poets and innumerable lectures. Spent one year in Berlin (1922–23), then returned to Russia.

Though a lesser poet than Blok, Bely was perhaps the most original and influential of the symbolists. A recognised master of metre and rhythm, he was also an important literary critic and an original theorist of Russian prosody.

BLOK, Alexander Alexandrovich, 1880–1921. Probably the greatest *poet* of the " silver age " of Russian literature, and of the symbolist movement; worshipped by young people in Russia before the revolution. Began writing very early. Contributed to symbolist journal *The Golden Fleece*. In 1904 published *Verses about the Beautiful Lady,* poems of mystical love for a being whom Blok identified with the feminine hypostasis of the Deity. Soon, however, his poetry became more pessimistic and more earthy. In " The Stranger " (1904–8) he is preoccupied with the social conflict and with the image of the Unknown Woman which has replaced that of the Beautiful Lady. The cycle "The Field of Kulikovo" (1908) shows Blok's sensitiveness to Russia's destiny, which verged on prophecy. He welcomed the Bolshevik revolution as a cleansing storm and as the expression of Russia's elemental soul. This concept found expression in his famous poem "The Twelve" (1918), an apocalyptic vision of the revolution personified by twelve Red Army men, apostles of the new world, led by Christ crowned with a wreath of white roses, and patrolling the streets of Petrograd. But Blok's enthusiasm soon waned. After "The Scythians" (written in January 1918 and expressing Russia's "love-hatred" of the West) he wrote little else and died, a disillusioned man, three years later.

BOBROV, Sergey Pavlovich, b. 1889. *Poet.* Leader of futurist "Centrifugue Group" and author of works on versification and theory of literature. His prose tale *The Revolt of the Misanthropes* is, like Zamyatin's more famous *We*, a horrifying vision of the collectivist future.

BRYUSOV, Valery Yakovlevich, 1873–1924. *Poet.* Born in Moscow, grandson of a serf, son of a rich merchant of radical views. Studied at Moscow University. In the 'nineties read Baudelaire, Verlaine, Mallarmé. In 1894–95 edited *Russian Symbolists.* In 1895 published his own poems, provocatively called *Chefs d'œuvres,* and was attacked as a decadent. Became editorial secretary to journal *Russian Archive* (1903), then to *New Way.* Worked with publishing firm Scorpion which published his *Tertia Vigilia* and *Urbi et Orbi.* Editor of journal *The Scales* published by Scorpion (1904–09) and literary editor of *Russian Thought* (1910–12). Became war correspondent in 1914. Wrote poem to Gorky in 1917. Joined Bolsheviks in 1919; founded Literary and Art Institute in 1921. Died of typhus. Published some eighty books in his lifetime, including translations of Verhaeren, Maeterlinck, E. A. Poe, Goethe, Virgil, etc., some historical novels, and works on Pushkin, Gogol, Tyutchev, etc. Introduced free verse into

Russian poetry and was the first to use peasant dance tune rhythm (*chastushki*). A cold academic poet who made important contributions to the technique of Russian prosody; Andrey Bely spoke of him as "the poet of marble and bronze".

CHIKOVANI, Simon Ivanovich, b. 1902. *Poet.* Glorified the revolution in Georgia. Awarded Stalin Prize in 1947.

DROZHZIN, Spiridon Dmitryevich, 1848–1930. *Poet.* Of peasant origin. Began publishing verse in 1873. From 1896 lived in his native village in Tver province, farming and writing. Influenced by Nekrasov. Depicted hardships of peasant life. Welcomed revolution. Wrote "In Memory of Lenin" (1924).

DURYLIN, Sergey Nikolayevich, b. 1881. *Poet. Critic.* Pseudonyms: S. Severny, S. Rayevsky. In 1916 wrote study on Lermontov from standpoint of Andrey Bely's theories. Important later books: *Repin and Garshin* (1926), *From Gogol's Family Chronicle* (1928), *About Tolstoy* (1928).

EHRENBURG, Ilya Grigoryevich, b. 1891. *Novelist.* In 1909 went to Paris and entered the bohemian literary world. First wrote poetry. During the First World War remained in France as war correspondent. Returned to Russia in 1917 and lived in the south under the Whites. In 1921 was arrested by the Soviet authorities, but released when cleared by them. Returned to Paris and stayed mostly in Western Europe until 1941. Was Soviet war correspondent in Spain in 1936–37. During Second World War wrote much patriotic propaganda. First successful novel, *Julio Jurenito* (1922), a satire. *Trust D. E.* (1923), a fantasy of the conquest of Europe by America. *The Second Day* (1933) depicts the construction of a steel works in Siberia and an intellectual's acceptance of Soviet life. His *Storm* and *Ninth Wave* were widely read in England and America. His novel *The Thaw*, written soon after Stalin's death, involved him in heated polemics with several Soviet writers, especially Konstantin Simonov.

ELLIS-KOBYLINSKY, Lev Lvovich, 1874–1947. *Poet* and *critic*. Member of Society of Religious Philosophy. Emigrated and died in Locarno.

ENGEL, Yuly Dmitryevich, 1868–1927. Leading *writer* on musical subjects and *composer*. Studied at Moscow Conservatoire. From 1897 in charge of music column in *Russian News*. One of the founders of the People's Conservatoire (1906) and of the Society for Jewish Folk Music (1908). First biographer of Scriabin (1916). After 1917 active in musical education. Emigrated to Tel-Aviv in 1924.

FADEYEV, Alexander Alexandrovich, 1901–56. *Novelist*. Of peasant origin, grew up in far eastern Siberia. Served on Red side in Civil War. First important work: short novel, *The Rout* (1927), set among partisans in Far East. *The Last of the Udegs* (1928–36) depicts changes made by revolution in the life of an almost extinct Far Eastern tribe. Wrote famous war novel *The Young Guard* (1945); re-wrote parts of it after strong Communist Party criticism. 1939–53: Secretary of Union of Soviet Writers. An ardent Stalinist, Fadeyev was strongly criticised by his fellow writers during the "thaw". He committed suicide in 1956.

FEDIN, Konstantin Alexandrovich, b. 1892. *Novelist*. Member of the Serapion Brotherhood, see below. *Cities and Years* (1924), was one of the earliest attempts to show the impact of the revolution on an intellectual and was attacked by some Soviet critics for its hero's "doubts". The hero of *Brothers* (1928) is an artist whose individualism is again opposed to the obligations of Soviet life. In the 'thirties Fedin appears to have overcome his objections to the Soviet régime. *The Rape of Europe* (1934) contrasts "decadent" Europe with progressive Russia. After the war published *Early Joys* (1945–46) and *Extraordinary Summer* (1948).

(*Serapion Brotherhood:* formed in 1921. Named after the hermit Serapion in Hoffman's *Tales,* in whose cave various people gathered and told their experiences. Besides Fedin the group included Tikhonov, Vsevolod Ivanov and others.

It helped to bring older writers in touch with younger writers demobilised from the Civil War, and to restore normal literary activity.)

GE (or Gué), Nikolay Nikolayevich, 1831–94. *Painter.* Studied in Italy. Member of Society for Travelling Art Exhibitions. Close friend of Tolstoy. Painted religious, then historic, scenes of great dramatic power (e.g. "The Last Supper", "Peter the Great and the Tsarevich Alexey"). His portraits include those of Turgenev, Nekrasov, Tolstoy, etc. Under Tolstoy's influence went back to religious themes (e.g. "What is Truth?", "Crucifixion", etc.).

GLIER, Reingold Moritsovich, 1874–1957. *Composer* and *conductor.* Born in Kiev of musical family. Studied at Kiev College of Music and Moscow Conservatoire. Began conducting in 1908. 1914–20: Director of Kiev College of Music; 1920–41: Director of Moscow Conservatoire. One of the most prominent figures in the Moscow post-revolutionary musical world. Composed ballets including *Red Poppy* (first ballet on revolutionary theme) and *Bronze Horseman.* People's Artist of the U.S.S.R. Awarded Order of Lenin and three Stalin Prizes. Prokofyev and other composers were his pupils.

GONCHAROVA, Natalya Sergeyevna, b. 1883. *Painter.* Influenced by cubism, futurism, Eastern folk art, Henri Rousseau. Married Larionov and tried, with him, to found new theory "Luchism" (*luch:* "ray"). Took part in "World of Art" exhibitions. Went to Paris on Diaghilev's invitation and was responsible for several of his settings including *Coq d'Or.* Exhibited in Paris and America.

GRIN, Alexander Stepanovich, pen-name of Grinevsky, 1880–1932. *Novelist.* Author of fantastic novels and short stories which enjoyed a tremendous popularity in the Soviet Union.

GUMILYOV, Nikolay Stepanovich, 1886–1921. *Poet.* Principal founder of acmeism (cf. note on AKHMATOVA). Studied in Paris and Petersburg. First book published in Paris in 1905. Married Akhmatova in 1910, divorced in 1918. In 1911 travelled in Abyssinia and Somaliland and remained fascinated by Africa. Only Russian poet to enlist as private in 1914; awarded St. George's Cross twice; commissioned in 1915. Was in Paris, as Provisional Government Commissioner for Affairs of Russian Troops in France, when October Revolution broke out; returned to Russia in 1918. Lived in Petrograd, taking part in work of translation initiated by Gorky, teaching younger poets and writing his best verse ("The Pyre", 1918, and "The Pillar of Fire", 1921). Shot for alleged participation in White Guard conspiracy. His poetry, exotic and fantastic, is dominated by his love of adventure.

IVANOV, Sergey Vasilyevich, 1846–1910. *Painter*. Member of Society for Travelling Art Exhibitions.

IVANOV, Vsevolod Vyacheslavovich, b. 1895. *Novelist* and *playwright*. Associated for a time with Serapion Brotherhood (cf. Note on FEDIN). Wrote on Civil War in which he had taken part (*Partisans,* 1921). His play, *Armoured Train* 14–69, was produced by Stanislavsky for Moscow Arts Theatre. Play, *Blockade* (1929), deals with suppression of Kronstadt rising of 1921. Returned to Civil War themes in the 'thirties, wrote patriotic articles and stories during Second World War, and in 1947 published *Encounters with Maxim Gorky*. (No relation to Vyacheslav Ivanov.)

IVANOV, Vyacheslav Ivanovich, 1866–1949. *Poet* and classical scholar of great erudition. Born in Moscow, son of a geodesist. Studied at Moscow University but left after two terms for Berlin where he studied history under Mommsen, as well as philology and philosophy. Travelled in Europe, Egypt and Palestine, lived mainly in Italy. The main subject of his research was the Cult of Dionysius and the Origins of Tragedy. Was influenced by Nietzsche and Vladimir Solovyov. Settled in Petersburg in 1905. Wrote for the journals, *Golden Fleece, The Scales, Apollo,* etc. After the revolution was active in education in Moscow, then became professor at Baku University. Emigrated in 1924. Became a Roman Catholic. Died in Rome. Wrote poetry and prose works of which some have been translated (e.g. *Freedom and the Tragic Life*, a study of Dostoyevsky).

KHLEBNIKOV, Velemir (Viktor) Vladimirovich, 1885–1922. *Poet.* Founder of Russian futurism and co-author of futurist manifesto, *A Slap in the Face of Public Taste* (cf. note on ASEYEV). One of the most eccentric and controversial figures of modern Russian literature. Born in Astrakhan, son of a civil servant. Came to Petersburg and joined *avant garde* literary circles in 1909. Travelled about Russia, his only luggage an old pillow-case stuffed with MSS. of his poems and calculations intended to establish mathematical laws in history. Served in Tsarist Army, then took part in Red Army campaign in Persia (1920); died in extreme poverty. Had great insight into spirit of Russian language; most modern poets have been influenced by his feeling for words. His first "etymological" poem (1910) consisted of nothing but invented derivatives of the word *smekh* (laughter).

KHODASEVICH, Vladislav Felitsyanovich, 1886–1939. *Poet, critic* and *literary historian.* Published his first poems in 1908 but won general recognition only after publication of post-revolutionary books, *The Way of the Grain* (1920) and *The Heavy Lyre* (1923). His poetry expresses contradiction between the freedom of man's immortal soul and its slavery to matter and necessity. A striking feature of his writing is his poetic wit. Emigrated in 1922, lived in Paris and became a brilliant literary critic and expert on Pushkin.

KLYUCHEVSKY, Vasily Osipovich, 1841–1911. Famous *historian.* Professor of Moscow University and at one time Leonid Pasternak's part-time colleague on the staff of the School of Painting, Sculpture and Architecture. His most important work: *Course of Russian History*, 5 vols., published 1904–11.

KOMISSARZHEVSKAYA, Vera Fyodorovna, 1864–1910. Famous dramatic *actress.* Began stage career as amateur in 1892; went to the provinces as professional actress in 1893. In 1896 joined the Petersburg Alexandrinsky Theatre. Founded her own theatre in Petersburg in 1904. Sister of famous producer Fyodor Komissarzhevsky.

KOROVIN, Konstantin Alexeyevich, 1861–1939. Landscape *painter*, but particularly famous as designer of scenery for theatre and opera, e.g. *A Life for the Tsar* (1904), *Sadko* (1906), *The Snow Maiden* (1907), *Khovanshchina* (1912). Later became an impressionist. Died in emigration.

KRYMOV, Nikolay Petrovich, b. 1884. *Painter*. Began as journalist, member of "Blue Rose" group. Later turned to realistic landscape painting. Also designed theatre décors.

LEONIDZE, Georgy Nikolayevich, b. 1899. *Poet*. At first influenced by symbolists. Wrote poems praising Socialist Construction; also about the countryside and history of Georgia. Awarded Stalin Prizes in 1941 and 1952.

LEVITAN, Isaak Ilyich, 1860–1900. *Painter*, famous for his poetic interpretation of Russian landscape. One of Chekhov's closest friends. Painted series of Volga scenes in the 'eighties and 'nineties. His "Vladimirka" (1892) shows the road followed by exiles to Siberia. In 1888 visited Paris where he discovered the Barbizon painters and impressionists and was influenced by their style.

LOMONOSOV, Mikhail Vasilyevich, 1711–65. *Poet* and *scientist*. Son of Archangel fisherman, ran away from home, walked to Moscow in search of education; rose to be a scientist of European fame. Head of Moscow University and poet of considerable merit; known as "father of modern Russian literature". Read mathematics, physics and philosophy at Marburg (1736–41) under Leibnitz's disciple, Christian Freiherr von Wolff (1679–1754). Wrote on Russian grammar and style.

MAKOVSKY, Sergey Konstantinovich, b. 1878. *Poet, critic* and editor of St. Petersburg review *Apollo* (1909–17). Emigrated in 1922. Lives in Paris.

MAKOVSKY, Vladimir Yegorovich, 1846–1920. *Painter*. Member of the Society for Travelling Art Exhibitions. Prominent in realist revolt against academism. Painted urban scenes emphasising social contrasts. Pictures include "The Condemned" (1879), "Bank Crash" (1881), "Interrogation of a Revolutionary" (1904).

MANDELSHTAMM, Osip Emilyevich, 1892–1942. Acmeist *poet*. Wrote only two small books of poems, *The Stone* (1916) and *Tristia* (1922); also essays on Russian civilisation and art of poetry. Had an extensive knowledge of Russian, French and Latin poetry; an original thinker and literary critic. An epigram about Stalin is said to have caused his deportation in the early 'thirties. He perished some time during the Second World War.

MARTYNOV, Leonid Nikolayevich, b. 1905. *Poet* and *journalist*. From 1922, published poems about the Civil War, and about Siberia and Central Asia where he has travelled.

MAYAKOVSKY, Vladimir Vladimirovich, 1893–1930. *Poet*. The most outstanding figure in Russian futurism (cf. note on ASEYEV). Born in Transcaucasia, son of a forestry official. Joined Bolshevik underground group at fourteen; spent some time in prison. Studied painting and joined newly emerging futurist movement whose revolutionary spirit and universalism attracted him. Signed Futurist Manifesto in 1912. In 1914 published tragedy, *Vladimir Mayakovsky*, in which he shocked the public by comparing himself to Christ. "The Cloud in Trousers" (1915) is a poem of unrequited love. In 1917 Mayakovsky rallied at once to the Soviet régime; wrote *Mystery Buffo* (1918), a verse play prophesying victory of revolution over capitalism. 1918–20: contributed drawings and texts for thousands of propaganda posters. In mid-'twenties travelled in Europe, U.S.A. and Latin America, writing poems sharply critical of life under capitalism. But his satirical plays, *The Red Bug* (1928) and *The Bath House* (1929), reflect disillusionment with growing philistinism and bureaucracy in Soviet life. Joined the Russian Association of Proletarian Writers (RAPP), the agency through which the Party controlled literature, and promised to write "a hundred Party books". But only two months later shot himself without having written another line except his suicide note, in which he said: " the boat of love has crashed on the rocks of everyday life. " Responsible communists always saw a dangerous individualism in his verse, but after his death his vogue as " the bard of the revolution " became an established cult.

MEDTNER, Emile Karlovich, 1872–1936. *Philosopher* and *philologist*. Emigrated and died in Dresden.

MURATOV, Pavel Pavlovich, 1881–1950. *Novelist* and *critic*. Associated with " The World of Art ". Author of *History of Old Russian Painting* (1914). Emigrated; lived in Dublin; published two books on *The Russian Campaigns* of 1941–43 and 1943–45, Penguin, 1941 and 1946.

MYASOYEDOV, Grigory Grigoryevich, 1835–1911. *Painter*. Studied abroad. On return to Russia became one of the organisers of the Society for Travelling Art Exhibitions. Paintings deal with peasant life and historical themes. Member of Academy of Art from 1893.

NADIRADZE, Kolau, b. 1894. Georgian *poet*. Studied at Moscow University. First verses appeared in 1916 in Georgian symbolist journal *Blue Horns* (cf. note on TABIDZE). His early poetry was mystical and nationalistic. After sovietisation of Georgia, Nadiradze was at first hostile but later wrote on revolutionary themes.

NILENDER, V. O. *Poet* and *translator*. Member of Society of Religious Philosophy.

OLENINA D'ALHEIM, Maria Alexeyevna, b. 1871. *Singer*. In 1908, founded Moscow music society *Dom Pesni* (" House of Song ") which played a notable role in the development of musical taste in Moscow and Petersburg. Wrote *The Legacy of Mussorgsky*. After 1918 lived in Paris. Married to French critic Pierre d'Alheim.

OSTROVSKY, Alexander Nikolayevich, 1823–86. Famous *playwright*, closely associated with the Maly Theatre in Moscow.

PASTERNAK, Boris Leonidovich, b. 1890. *Poet* and *novelist*. Born in Moscow, son of painter Leonid Pasternak and pianist Rosa Pasternak, née Kaufman. 1890–1901: childhood in Moscow with frequent visits to paternal grandparents in Odessa. 1901: enters secondary school in Moscow. Summer 1903: meeting with Scriabin opens period of intense preoccupation with music. 1906: first visit abroad (family spent a year in Berlin). 1908: enters Moscow University (Faculty of Law). 1909: Scriabin returns to Russia; on his advice Pasternak changes over from law to philosophy. 1910–12: frequents the "Serdarda" circle and the *Musaget* group of writers, poets and critics. Summer 1912: spends summer term at Marburg University reading neo-Kantian philosophy under Hermann Cohen. Has an abortive love affair. Discovers poetry as his true vocation and abandons philosophy. Visits Venice and Florence. Spring 1913: graduates from Moscow University. Summer 1913: first period of active poetic work. Spring 1914: joins the "Centrifugue", an association of moderate futurists. May 1914: meets Mayakovsky. Autumn 1914: publishes first collection of verse, *The Twin in the Clouds* (*Bliznets v tuchakh*). 1914–16: tutor to son of a Moscow manufacturer. October 1915: meets Khlebnikov, founder of Russian futurism. 1915–17: spends two winters doing clerical work in ordnance factories in the Urals. March 1917: returns to Moscow. Publishes second book of verse, *Above the Barriers* (*Poverkh baryerov*); writes (and loses MS. of) *The Reverse of the Medal* (*Oborotnaya storona medali*). Summer 1917: writes third book of verse *My Sister, Life* (*Sestra moya zhizn*). 1918: writes two short stories *The Childhood of Luvers* and *Letters from Tula.* Winter 1918–19: severe illness. 1920: estrangement from Mayakovsky. May 1921: meets Alexander Blok in Moscow. 1921: Pasternak's parents and sisters leave for Berlin. Pasternak works as salesman in Writers' Bookshop in Moscow. Comes across Tsvetayeva's poetry. Publishes *My Sister, Life* which establishes his poetic reputation. 1922: marries; goes with his wife to Berlin to visit his parents and prepare publication of fourth book of verse; revisits Marburg. 1923: birth of his son. In January reads his verse at the Writers' Club in Berlin. Publishes (simultaneously in Berlin and Moscow) his fourth collection of verse, *Themes and Variations* (*Temy i varyatsii*). Returns to Moscow in the autumn. 1924: short spell of work in library of People's Commissariat of Foreign Affairs. 1925: publication of four short stories in book form. (*Childhood of Luvers*, *Letters from Tula*, *Il Tratto di Apelle*, *Aerial Ways*.) 1927: publication in book form of two historical poems, *The Year Nineteen hundred and five* and *Lieutenant Schmidt*. 1927: publication of *Povest* (" A Story "); 1927–36: Pasternak's poetry acquires great popularity in Russia and is published and republished in various editions. 1929–31: serialisation of Pasternak's first autobiography, *Safe Conduct* (*Okhrannaya Gramota*). 1930–31: friendship with Paolo Yashvili. Early 1930's: divorce and remarriage. Stay in Georgia. Work on translations of Georgian poets. 1931: publication of novel in verse *Spektorsky*, and of a collection of verse for children, *The Zoo*. 1932: publication of collected poems, *Second Birth* (*Vtoroye rozhdenye*). 1932–41: silence as a poet. Active work as translator. August 1934: first Congress of Union of Soviet Writers; Pasternak praised and attacked but generally regarded as master of modern Russian poetry. Middle 1930's: Pasternak moves to his present home at Peredelkino. June 1935: attends first Anti-Fascist Congress of Writers in Paris. Meets Tsvetayeva and her family. 1937: refuses to sign document approving of execution of Tukhachevsky and others. 1937: befriends young playwright Alexander Afinogenov who was expelled from the Party and from the Union of Soviet Writers. 1935–37: publication in book form of translations of Georgian poets. 1941: translation of *Hamlet* published. 1941–45: publishes patriotic war poems and continues work on translations of Shakespeare. 1942: translation of *Romeo and Juliet* published. 1943: publication of collected poems *In Early Trains* (*Na rannikh poyezdakh*). 1944: translation of *Antony and Cleopatra* published. 1945: translation of *Othello* published. Publication of collected poems *Wide Spaces of the Earth* (*Zemnye prostory*). 1946:

Zhdanov's savage attack on " cosmopolitanism " in literature imposes renewed silence on Pasternak as a poet. 1950: publication of translations of Goethe's *Faust* and of selected poems by Petöfi. April 1954: publishes ten poems from *Doctor Zhivago* in the journal *Znamya,* and announces novel. Summer 1956: submits MS. of novel, *Doctor Zhivago,* to editorial board of *Novy Mir*. September 1956: editors of *Novy Mir* reject novel. Autumn 1957: *Doctor Zhivago* first published abroad in Italian. Some poems appear in *Novy Mir*.

PASTERNAK, Leonid Iosifovich, 1862–1945. Well-known *painter* and *illustrator*. Father of Boris Pasternak. Left Russia in 1921 and, while retaining his Soviet citizenship, lived first in Germany (Berlin and Munich) and, from 1938, in England. Died in Oxford.

PASTERNAK, Rosa Isidorovna, née Kaufman, 1867–1940. *Pianist*. Her talent was discovered by Anton Rubinstein who sponsored several of her concert tours. Gave up professional career on marriage. Mother of Boris Pasternak.

PETROVSKY, Mikhail Alexeyevich, b. 1887. *Critic* and *translator*.

PILNYAK, Boris Andreyevich, pen-name of Vogau, 1894–1937. *Novelist*. First works published in 1915. Novel *The Bare Year* (1922) deals with Civil War and shows life degraded to animal level. *Tale of the Unextinguished Moon* (1926) hints that death on the operating table of War Commissar Frunze (1925) was a " medical murder " ordered by Stalin. *Mahogany* was refused publication in Russia and Pilnyak had it published in Berlin in 1929. This led to his expulsion from the Union of Soviet Writers. In 1937 he disappeared and is believed to have been shot. He was partly rehabilitated posthumously after Stalin's death.

POLENOV, Vasily Dmitryevich, 1844–1927. *Painter*. Paintings of country life. War artist in Russo-Turkish War of 1877–78. Member of Society for Travelling Art Exhibitions. Painted scenes from the life of Christ (1880's). Elected member of Academy of Art in 1893. After revolution lived in a village now called Polenovo.

PRZYBYSZEWSKI, Stanislaw, 1868–1927. Outstanding Polish *poet* and *playwright*. Wrote plays full of fatalistic terror and poems on the mystical and tragic aspects of love and death, which became very fashionable.

RACHINSKY, Grigory Alexeyevich. One of the moving spirits of the Society of Religious Philosophy. Professor at Moscow University. An advocate of children's religious education.

REBIKOV, Vladimir Ivanovich, 1866–1920. *Composer*. One of the first representatives of modernism in Russian music. A " miniaturist " in music, influenced by impressionism and symbolism, he composed *Fables* based on Krylov and the opera *Christmas Tree* based on Dostoyevsky. Believed in a system of music and mimics which he called " melo-mimics ".

REPIN, Ilya Yefimovich, 1844–1930. Famous *painter*. Studied in Petersburg, Italy and Paris. Active in the Society for Travelling Art Exhibitions. Paintings deal with peasant life and historical subjects, e.g. " Ivan the Terrible with his Son " (1885), " The Zaporozhian Cossacks write to the Sultan " (1891). Portraits include those of Tolstoy and other well-known writers and artists and, among foreign celebrities, Eleonora Duse.

SADOVSKY, Boris Alexandrovich, b. 1881. Symbolist *poet* and *critic*.

SAPUNOV, Nikolay Nikolayevich, 1880–1912. *Painter*. Studied under Levitan, Korovin, Serov. Visited Italy in 1902. Joined " Blue Rose " group. Painted landscapes: designed scenery for productions of Ibsen's *Hedda Gabler,* Blok's *Balaganchik*, Gozzi's *Turandot,* etc.

SCRIABIN, Alexander Nikolayevich, 1872–1915. *Composer*. Born in Moscow, son of diplomat and pianist. Attended Cadet School. Studied at Moscow Conservatoire (1882–92), winning a Gold Medal as a pianist. 1898–1903: Professor of Piano at Moscow Conservatoire. Early compositions show kinship with Chopin. *Poème Satanique* (1903) echoes Liszt's *Malédiction* and shows Scriabin committing himself to magical view of art. His first symphony (1901) already showed taste for the grandiose; with his fourth piano sonata (1903) he throws off the drawing-room elegance of his early compositions and develops the fragmentation of melody and the ecstatic trills of his maturer period. His idea of music as incantation is explicit in the inscription on the orgiastic fifth piano sonata: " I call you forth to life, hidden influences sunk in the obscure depths of the Creative Spirit, timid germs of life, I bring you boldness! " Scriabin became interested in theosophy and saw himself as the messiah destined to bring about "Final Act", the act of Union between the Male-Creator and the Female World", by which Spirit was to redeem matter, a great liturgical rite in which all the arts would play their part and which would usher in a new era. Attempted approach to his idea in *Prometheus* " fire poem " for orchestra, piano and *clavier à lumière;* the latter was a first attempt to achieve synthesis of the arts and " counterpoint of the senses ": he dreamed of " a musical phrase ending in a scent, a chord resolving itself into colour, a melodic line whose climax is a caress ". His most famous composition: *Poème de l'extase*. 1904–10: toured Switzerland, France (where he became acquainted with writings of Madame Blavatsky and Annie Besant), Italy and U.S.A. In 1910 performed in Holland and in 1914 in Britain. In 1922 his flat in Moscow was made a museum.

SELVINSKY, Ilya Lvovich, b. 1899. *Poet.* Leader of Constructivists (cf. below). At one time looked like taking Mayakovsky's place. Published first poems in 1926. Of his later works his ballads and songs were the most successful. Wrote poem about Arctic expedition of Chelyuskin in which he had taken part (1933–34). Wrote patriotic verses during 1941–45 war.

(*Constructivists:* a group of young poets organised in 1924. Took over futurists' (cf. note on ASEYEV) interest in technology and other contemporary themes but were less anti-traditional. Believed that a poem should be a " construction " in which, as in engineering, the maximum effect is derived from a given potential. In 1929–30 the group rallied a number of poets to active support of the régime. Broke up in 1930.)

SEROV, Valentin Alexandrovich, 1865–1911. *Painter.* Born in Petersburg, son of composers A. N. Serov and V. S. Serova. Pupil of Repin. Mainly distinguished as portrait painter but also painted scenes of country life and dramatic compositions, e.g. " The Meeting: Arrival of an Exile's Wife ". At the end of nineteenth century joined " World of Art " group. During 1905 revolution drew caricatures for the revolutionary press. Protested to Academy of Arts against massacre of 9th January and resigned from Academy when protest was rejected. Portraits include Chaliapin and Stanislavsky. In last years of his life was influenced by contemporary French painting (e.g. his portrait of Ida Rubinstein).

SEVERYANIN, Igor, pen-name of Igor Vasilyevich Lotaryev, 1887–1941. *Poet.* Member of so-called " Ego-Futurists ". Facile command of rhythm; vocabulary of modern city life and technology; profuse coining of new words; but had little to express save cheap dreams of luxury and sensuality. Extremely popular after publication of his " Thunder-Seething Cup " (1913). Emigrated; was in Esthonia when it was occupied by the Soviet Union in 1940 and wrote verses greeting the Soviet power.

SHCHEGOLEV, Pavel Yeliseyevich, 1877–1931. *Literary historian.*

SHENROK, Vladimir Ivanovich, 1853–1910. *Literary historian.* Specialised in Gogol.

SHERSHENEVICH, Vadim Gabrielevich, 1893–1942. *Poet.* At first influenced by symbolism, later by futurism, then by imagism (cf. below). Wrote verses which are almost disconnected lists of metaphors. Translator of Shakespeare, Corneille, Baudelaire. Wrote film scenarios, libretti for operettas, etc.

(*Imagism:* A poetic movement organised in 1909 which stressed imagery and metaphor as basis of poetry. Favoured free verse. Introduced coarsest images side by side with the pathetic and the sublime. The imagists in Moscow led a rowdy bohemian life and boasted of their hooliganism. After 1924 the group fell apart.)

SIMONOV, Konstantin Mikhaylovich, b. 1915. *Poet, novelist, playwright.* Early verse mostly love poetry. Graduated from literary institute of Union of Soviet Writers in 1938. Wrote a patriotic poem about Suvorov in 1939. During Second World War became the most famous lyric poet. Wrote war novels: *Days and Nights, Comrades in Arms,* and plays including the anti-American play *The Russian Question.* Since the war mainly active in journalism as editor of *Literaturnaya Gazeta* and *Novy Mir.*

SOLOVYOV, Vladimir Sergeyevich, 1853–1900. *Poet, critic* and most influential Russian nineteenth-century *religious philosopher.*

SOMOV, Konstantin Nikolayevich, 1869–1939. *Painter* and *art critic.* Member of " World of Art " group.

STASOV, Vladimir Vasilyevich, 1824–1906. Art and music *critic.* Keen supporter of the Society for Travelling Art Exhibitions. In 1880's wrote number of books on history of art. Edited published letters of Musorgsky and Glinka.

STEPUN, Fyodor Avgustovich, b. 1884. Stage *producer, writer* and scholar. Author of several novels and of an autobiography which gives an excellent picture of the artistic and literary atmosphere in pre-revolutionary Moscow. Emigrated, lives in Germany.

SUDEYKIN, Sergey Yuryevich, b. 1883. *Painter.* Took part in " Blue Rose " and " World of Art " exhibitions. Mainly landscapes, studies for theatre scenery. Exhibited in Paris, 1921.

SURIKOV, Vasily Ivanovich, 1848–1916. *Painter.* Member of Society for Travelling Art Exhibitions. Studied in Petersburg but quarrelled with his conservative professors and moved to Moscow (1877). Vast historical pictures: " The Morning of the Execution of the Strelsy " (1881), " The Boyarina Morozova " (1887), scenes from lives of Stenka Razin, Pugachev, etc.

TABIDZE, Titsian Yustinovich, 1895–1937. Georgian *poet.* Studied at Moscow University. Was one of the founders of the "Blue Horns" group of Georgian symbolist poets (1915). Rallied to Soviet régime after 1921 and helped to found Union of Georgian Writers. At the Congress of Soviet writers in 1934 the Blue Horns group was criticised by the chairman of the Union of Georgian Writers as still being only "fellow-travellers". Tabidze perished in one of the purges in the 'thirties.

TIKHONOV, Nikolay Semyonovich, b. 1896. *Poet.* Fought in First World War and on Red side in Civil War. Wrote war poems 1916–17. Next two books of poems, *The Horde* and *Country Beer* came out in 1922. *The Shadow of a Friend* includes poems written in Poland, Austria, France, Belgium and England, while *Yurga* and *Poems of Kakhetia* are about his experiences in the Caucasus and Central Asia. He is attracted by strong personalities, grandiose scenery and dangerous undertakings. His experiences in beleaguered Leningrad are described in his war poems, *The Fiery Year.*

TIKHONOV, A. N. Editor of *Russky Sovremennik,* a periodical in which Pasternak published works in poetry and prose in the 'twenties.

TOLSTOY, Alexey Konstantinovich, 1817–1875. *Poet* and *dramatist.* The Moscow Arts Theatre opened its first season (October 1898) with his play, *Tsar Fyodor Ivanovich.*

TOLSTOY, Andrey Lvovich, 1877–1916. Leo Tolstoy's third son.

TOLSTOY, Ilya Lvovich, 1866–1933. Author of *Reminiscences of my Father.* Leo Tolstoy's second son.

TOLSTOY, Sergey Lvovich, 1863–1947. Leo Tolstoy's eldest son, author of monograph, *My Father in the Seventies.*

TRETYAKOV, Sergey Mikhailovich, 1892–1947. *Playwright.* Author of *Roar, China!* produced by Meyerhold. Disappeared during purges of 1937–38.

TRUBETSKOY, Prince Nikolay Sergeyevich, 1890–1938. Emigrated in 1920 and became professor of comparative philology at the University of Vienna, a post which he held from 1923 until his death.

TRUBETSKOY, Prince Pavel (Paolo) Petrovich, 1867–1938. *Sculptor.* Born and died in Italy. Worked in France and U.S.A. Except for brief visits between 1907 and 1914, lived in Russia only from 1897–1906, and hardly knew Russian. A brilliant sculptor of impressionist tendencies, he excelled in equestrian subjects. Works include " Tolstoy on Horseback " (1899) and equestrian monument to Alexander III unveiled in Petersburg in 1909.

TRUBETSKOY, Prince Sergey Nikolayevich, 1862–1905. Leading *philosopher.* Took active part in liberal opposition in 1904–05. Died soon after being elected Rector of Moscow University.

TRUBETSKOY, Prince Yevgeny Nikolayevich, 1863–1920. Brother of Sergey. Taught theory of law at Moscow University. As political writer fought a hopeless battle against the two " apocalyptic beasts of reaction and revolution."

TSVETAYEVA, Marina Ivanovna, 1892–1941. *Poetess.* Began literary work in 1910. Left Russia in 1922 to join her husband Yefron who, after fighting as White officer in Civil War, was evacuated with remnants of Wrangel's army to Constantinople and later found his way to Prague. The family (there were a son and daughter) lived in reduced circumstances in Prague, then in Paris. In 1939 they decided to return to Russia (Yefron after fighting on Republican side in the Spanish Civil War). On their return Yefron was arrested and perished; the daughter was also arrested; the son was killed at the front early in the war. Tsvetayeva herself was banished to a provincial town, Yelabuga, where she could not find work —even as a charwoman—and hanged herself on 31st August, 1941.

TVARDOVSKY, Alexander Trifonovich, b. 1910. *Poet.* First poems appeared in 1930. Achieved fame with three long narrative poems, " The Land of Muravia," " Vasily Tvorkin " and " The House by the Roadside." Highly imaginative realism.

TYUTCHEV, Fyodor Ivanovich, 1803–73. Lyric *poet.* Served in Diplomatic Service (1822–39) and in Censorship Department (1844–73). Poetic production small (about three hundred short poems). Striking use of colloquialism against background of formal eighteenth-century vocabulary. Certain lines from Tyutchev's nature poetry read like anticipations of Pasternak.

ULYANOV, Nikolay Pavlovich, 1875–1949. *Painter.* Studied under Serov. Portraits include those of Chekhov and Stanislavsky. Did much theatre work including settings for *Les fourberies de Scapin, Carmen,* etc. His memoirs were published posthumously in 1952.

VASNETSOV, Appollinary Mikhailovich, 1856–1933. *Painter.* Born in Northern Russia, son of a village priest. Joined Society for Travelling Art Exhibitions and became well known as landscape painter, especially of Urals and Siberian scenes. From 1890 lived in Moscow and painted pictures of its historic past. Elected to Academy in 1900. Designed scenery for operas *Khovanshchina, Sadko,* etc. Attacked impressionism.

VASNETSOV, Victor Mikhailovich, 1848–1926. *Painter.* Elder brother of Appollinary. Associated with Repin and V. V. Stasov. In 1878 moved to Moscow. Painted subjects from Russian folk-lore and medieval history, e.g. "Ivan the Terrible" and "Bogatyri" (often reproduced).

VERHAEREN, Emile. 1855–1916. Belgian *poet.* Influenced by impressionist painting.

VRUBEL, Mikhail Alexandrovich, 1856–1910. *Painter.* Member of Academy from 1905 on. Well known as book illustrator and theatrical designer.

YASHVILI, Paolo Dzhibraelovich, 1895–1937. Georgian *poet.* Went to Paris on eve of First World War. On his return in 1916 became a leader of the "Blue Horns" group (cf. note on TABIDZE). During Menshevik occupation in Georgia (1918–21) his poetry reflected ardent Georgian nationalism. But he is said to have welcomed the establishment of Soviet rule and wrote a poem on Lenin's death and in praise of socialist construction. Translated Pushkin, Lermontov and Mayakovsky into Georgian. Committed suicide.

YESENIN, Sergey Alexandrovich. 1895–1925. Great lyric *poet.* Born in Central Russia, son of a peasant. Went to parish school, then studied at a free University in Moscow while working as printer's reader. Went to Petrograd, met Blok there and decided to stay. Welcomed revolution, especially for what he hoped it would do for peasants, but was disillusioned by Bolshevik proletarisation and industrialisation of country life. Joined imagists in 1919 (cf. note on SHERSHENEVICH) and took part in their rowdy café life. Married Isadora Duncan in 1922 and went abroad with her; they separated a year later and he returned to Russia. Suffered a mental breakdown and in December 1925 cut his wrists, wrote a farewell poem in his own blood and hanged himself. Particularly memorable for his earliest and latest poems evoking Russian countryside. Enjoyed enormous popularity in his lifetime, particularly with the younger generation.

ZABOLOTSKY, Nikolay, b. 1903. *Poet* and *translator.* Early poems sound like parodies or nonsense verse. Disappeared for several years and re-emerged fairly recently, writing in more orthodox style. Works include translation in verse of twelfth-century epic, *The Lay of Prince Igor's Campaigns.*

12. Martin Luther—Parish Educator

1. *Geschichte des deutschen Volkes seit dem Ausgang des Mittelalters* (Freibourg, 1879), I, 289.
2. *History of Education* (Washington: Catholic University Press, 1915), p. 154.
3. *Dr. Martin Luthers Sämtliche Schriften,* hrsg. von Johann Georg Walch (Halle: Johann Justinus Gebauer, 1740-1749), X, 2. Hereafter referred to as *Walch.*
4. *Walch* X, 498.
5. *Walch* X, 537 f.
6. John Osborne, *Luther* (London: Faber and Faber, 1961), pp. 53 f.
7. *Walch* X, 198.
8. *Walch* XXII, 1785.
9. *Walch* X, 557.
10. *Walch* X, 502.
11. J. Michael Reu, *Catechetics* (3rd ed.; Chicago: Wartburg, 1931), p. 99.
12. (Minneapolis: Augsburg, 1928.)
13. (Philadelphia: Lutheran Publication Society, 1889.)
14. Arthur Cushman McGiffert, *Martin Luther: the Man and His Work* (New York: Century, 1911), p. 316.

13. Luther, Man of Prayer

1. Heino O. Kadai, ed., *Accents in Luther's Theology* (St. Louis: Concordia, 1967).
2. Julius Köstlin, *Luthers Theologie* (2 vols.; Stuttgart, 1863).
3. Paul Althaus, *The Theology of Luther* (Philadelphia: Fortress Press, 1966), p. 132.
4. Heinrich Bornkamm, *Luther's World of Thought* (St. Louis: Concordia, 1958), pp. 80 f.
5. Roland H. Bainton, *Here I Stand* (Nashville: Abingdon-Cokesbury Press, 1950), p. 358.
6. *Luthers Werke* (Berlin: C. A. Schwetschke und Sohn, 1905), VIII, p. 163.
7. Bainton, *Here I Stand,* p. 195.
8. Herbert F. Brokering, *Luther's Prayers* (Minneapolis: Augsburg 1967), Preface.
9. Julius Köstlin, *Martin Luther, Sein Leben und seine Schriften* II (Berlin: Alexander Duncker, 1903), p. 500.
10. *Ibid.,* I, 423.
11. *Ibid.,* II, 388.
12. *Ibid.,* II, 219.
13. *Ibid.,* II, 5.
14. *Ibid.,* II, 402.
15. *BC,* p. 291.
16. Köstlin, *Martin Luther* II, 526 f.
17. *LW* 48, 126.
18. *LW* 48, 256, 324.
19. *LW* 48, 215.
20. *LW* 48, 263.
21. *LW* 48, 372.
22. *LW* 48, 216.
23. *LW* 48, 235.
24. *LW* 48, 257.
25. Köstlin, *Martin Luther* II, 173.
26. *Luthers Werke* VI, 121.
27. *Ibid.,* I, 50.
28. *BC,* pp. 352-354.
29. *BC,* p. 352.
30. *BC,* pp. 358-362, particularly page 359.
31. *BC,* pp. 420-436.
32. *Luthers Werke* VI, pp. 125-146.
33. *Ibid.,* p. 132.
34. *Ibid.,* pp. 146-148.
35. *Ibid.,* V, p. 251
36. *Service Book and Hymnal,* No. 372.
37. *Ibid.,* No. 122.
38. *Ibid.,* No. 155.
39. *LW* 53, No. 291.
40. Köstlin, *Martin Luther* II, 622-624.